THE

ANXIOUS

HEART

Copyright © Aurum Technologies LLC 2023
E-mail: aurum.publishing1@gmail.com

All rights reserved. No part of this publication may be reproduced, distributed, or transmitted in any form or by any means, including photocopying, recording, or other electronic or mechanical methods, without the prior written permission of the publisher, except in the case of brief quotations embodied in critical reviews and certain other non-commercial uses permitted by copyright law.

While every effort has been made to ensure the accuracy of the information contained herein, the author and publisher assume no responsibility for errors, inaccuracies, or omissions. Any legal or technical information is for general informational purposes only and should not be considered as professional advice. Readers are encouraged to consult with relevant experts or authorities in specific fields for advice or guidance.

ISBN-13: 979-8868177781

Table of Contents

Introduction _____ 1

Chapter One: Attachment Styles and How They Correlate ___ 4

Chapter Two: A Deep Dive into Anxious Attachment _____ 21

Chapter Three: Anxious Attachment and Your Relationship _ 38

Chapter Four: Defining Boundaries and Independence ____ 58

Chapter Five: How to Change Your Behavior for Good with Cognitive Behavioral Therapy _____ 75

Chapter Six: Schema Therapy - An Effective Tool to Combat Anxious Attachment _____ 103

Chapter Seven: The Power of Affirmations and Visualization 117

Chapter Eight: Guided Meditation: The Path to Transforming Your Anxious Attachment _____ 141

Conclusion _____ 149

Author's Note _____ 157

References _____ 159

Introduction

Are you among the countless individuals who have ever felt an overwhelming fear of abandonment, a need for constant reassurance, or the inability to break free from a relationship that you know is toxic? Are you yearning for love and connection with a passion that borders on obsession or are you one of those who give more of yourself to others - often at the expense of your own mental or physical well-being? You can rest assured that these emotional patterns of anxious attachment and codependency are by no means uncommon or even unchangeable.

The human psyche is a puzzling and often confusing thing to understand, with emotions, desires, and vulnerabilities being just a few of the threads that are woven together to create the fabric of life. But what are anxious attachment and codependency, and just how can you go about identifying these patterns in yourself or a loved one and heal from them?

In the pages of this book you'll discover how to:

1. Identify anxious attachment and codependency through stories and relatable examples to help you recognize the signs and symptoms of these patterns and how they relate to your own life.

2. Understand the root cause of both anxious attachment and codependency as we delve into your childhood and other relationships. By understanding the root cause, you gain the power to heal.

3. Cultivate self-compassion as you go on a journey towards both self-acceptance and self-love. One of the key things you'll learn is that nurturing your own well-being is not selfish, but necessary to form and maintain healthy relationships.

4. Set healthy boundaries to help you protect and maintain your emotional and mental health while fostering meaningful connections with your friends and loved ones.

5. Help your loved ones heal. This book is as much for you as it is for them as it can help you develop the tools needed to offer support and encouragement on the path to recovery.

6. Tackle your anxious attachment head-on with tools like CBT techniques, daily affirmations, and guided meditation to learn actionable steps to permanently change your behavior and create the relationship you want and deserve. Partners and family members can also aid in supporting your journey using these techniques.

As we embark on this journey together, it is vital to remember that healing is not a destination, but a journey of self-discovery, compassion, and a little self-liberation. By understanding anxious attachment and codependency, you can take the first step toward breaking free from the shackles of these emotional patterns that are holding you back and create healthy, loving relationships with those around you.

So, without further ado, let's dive head first into the unknown waters that come with anxious attachment and codependency and teach you all you need to know to build a better future for yourself or your loved ones who suffer from these emotional patterns.

You've got this!

Chapter One: Attachment Styles and How They Correlate

◯✦◯

We've all felt a little unhinged at one time or another, right? And, no, we're not talking about those instances where we feel completely overwhelmed by life and everything that might be going on. We are talking specifically about that unsettling feeling we get in a relationship sometimes where we have to fight against the voices in our head telling us that our partner is going to up and leave at any minute.

This is pretty normal, but for people with anxious attachment or another unhealthy attachment style, it is an overriding fear that completely consumes them and is likely on their mind every minute of the day. So what is an insecure attachment? And why are some more prone to it than others?

As much as we want to say that there is an easy answer - or cure - for anxious attachment and all its intricacies, there isn't. Just as there is no definitive definition for this emotional pattern, there is no quick fix.

To understand what insecure attachments entail, let's take a quick look at the most common signs and symptoms of those who suffer from anxious attachment:

- A deep fear of abandonment
- Need for constant reassurance that all is well and that they are loved
- Strong desire for intimacy - more than others
- Doubts that relationships will work out
- Difficulty trusting others
- Often seen as clingy or needy in all relationships

We'll go into detail on these a bit more later on. Acknowledging and understanding these signs is the first step to making the necessary changes and learning how to cope with your anxious attachment before it takes over your life and your relationship. Accountability is key if you want to overcome your anxious attachment and change your behaviors for good.

What Is an Attachment?

It seems we have jumped ahead a bit and gone straight to the juicy part of this chapter as we have looked at the signs of an anxious attachment. To better understand the intricacies and behaviors associated with anxious attachment, we should first define what it really is.

An attachment is, in essence, an emotional bond that you form with another person, be it a partner, friend, or family member.

An insecure attachment is one where you fail to form secure and healthy attachments early in life that go on to negatively impact your behavior later in life. This is not your fault, but is rather a response to the care, or lack thereof, that you received in your early years. Anxious attachment is a perfect example of an insecure attachment, whereby your emotional needs or behaviors cause problems in a number of your relationships.

The Four Attachment Styles

There are four attachment styles that influence how we approach relationships with others.

1. **Anxious or preoccupied attachment.** People who adopt this attachment style fear abandonment and tend to be very clingy or needy in their relationships. This attachment style typically develops when our caregivers are inconsistent in meeting our emotional needs as children, but it can also be a result of a traumatic experience or relationship. This, in turn, makes it difficult for those who suffer from anxious attachment to cope with stress, as their fear of abandonment only intensifies during challenging or trying times. We'll look at anxious attachment in more detail in chapter two as we explore the effects of anxious attachment on the various

relationships we have with our partners, friends, and family members.

2. **Avoidant or dismissive attachment.** People who are dismissive in their attachment style do not feel the need for validation nor seek reassurance from others in a relationship. They are independent in nature, and do not necessarily go out of their way to form bonds with others. This attachment style is thought to develop when caregivers are emotionally distant or completely unavailable, and results in the individual learning to suppress their emotional needs rather than face them. Avoidant attachment individuals tend to cope with stress or stressful situations by withdrawing from them completely, leading to even further isolation.

3. **Disorganized or fearful-avoidant attachment.** This attachment style is characterized by difficulty in regulating emotions and avoiding emotional attachments with others. Disorganized attachment usually develops when caregivers are a source of both comfort and fear, resulting in conflicting emotions where the individual learns to associate that relationship with both safety and danger. Those with disorganized attachment often exhibit unpredictable and erratic behavior and may desire and fear intimacy in their

romantic relationships which can lead to confusion and a number of mixed signals.

4. **Secure attachment.** A secure attachment style is the one that we all hope for. 50 to 60% of the adult population have a secure attachment style, characterized by a healthy balance of independence and intimacy. People who adopt the secure attachment style openly express their emotions while also allowing others to rely on them. Secure attachments are the result of consistent and responsive meeting of one's emotional needs in one's younger years, leading to trust and the belief that one is worthy of love and care. Secure individuals are far better at handling any stress or adversity they may face in life, and have a secure base they can turn to for support.

It is worth repeating that no attachment style is fixed, and that you can evolve over time with self-awareness and a good self-help plan. Take control of your life as you identify your attachment style, learn what your triggers are, and commit to making the changes necessary to improve your life and your relationships. Everyone deserves a happy, meaningful relationship where they are loved and feel supported.

Attachment Theory and Anxious Attachment: What's the Link?

Anxious attachment was first explored in the '50s by British psychologist John Bowlby who, through his work on attachment theory, identified that anxious attachment likely stemmed from a failure to form secure attachments early in life.

Based on his now-famous model, from birth to 10 months plus was the critical age range within which humans develop these attachments, and went on to state that an insecure or anxious attachment was likely the result of a poorly formed emotional bond with a primary caregiver.

While it would be easy to blame all your current relationship problems on your parents, or how you were treated as a child, at some point or another you'll need to understand that your anxious attachment style is more likely due to some of your emotional needs not being met correctly, rather than your parents not loving you enough. As we have said before, it can also be a result of some other trauma that puts into motion a rather unhealthy way of viewing your self-worth in your relationships.

Let's look at Dr. Bowlby's theory in more detail by analyzing the four attachment stages he laid out in his theory, and how they relate to your relationships today.

The Four Stages of Attachment

Stage one: Pre-Attachment

This stage takes place from birth to around six weeks, and is characterized by no attachment to any specific caregiver.

Stage two: Indiscriminate Attachment

The second attachment stage takes place from six weeks of age until around seven months, and is when a baby starts to show preference to a primary or secondary caregiver.

Stage three: Discriminate Attachment

This all-important stage takes place from around seven months, and should be when the child shows a strong attachment to one parent or caregiver.

Stage four: Multiple Attachment

The last stage of Bowlby's attachment theory takes place from ten months, and has the child forming emotional bonds with other caregivers and family members.

It is all good and well for me to lay out the various attachment styles, but how do they actually relate to anxious attachment?

How would the bonds you form with your caregivers shortly after birth affect your attachment style later on?

Here is the answer: if your attachment needs were not met at each stage of development according to Bowlby's attachment theory, you might find yourself unable to:

- Communicate your emotions and needs to your partner, family, or friends
- Calmly and coherently respond to conflict situations
- Form unrealistic expectations about your relationships with the people in your life

Anxious attachment is just one of the results of not having your attachment needs met, and is most often caused by a difference in parenting styles or behaviors, and inconsistent parenting in which one or both of the parents or caregivers were not often present.

Bowlby's research into anxious attachment and attachment theory is by no means the final word on the matter as we also need to make mention of Rudolph Schaffer and Peggy Emerson's research conducted in 1964.

Their research is fairly similar to Bowlby's, which focuses on the root causes of anxious attachment stemming from a child's emotional needs not being met by their primary caregiver. Schaffer and Emerson's research, however, suggests that children form different bonds with different caregivers and that they form bonds with their mothers first and other caregivers later.

The main difference between the two is that Bowlby's suggest that all attachment styles are formed in infancy, which is not the case according to Emerson and Schaffer.

Someone who suffers from anxious attachment may come across as clingy or needy in the relationship, often pushing their partner further away. This is, of course, the opposite of what they want, but they are unable to understand their behaviors and desires. They are simply filling the gap that was left open when they were younger, and this, too, takes a lot of hard work and actually admitting that there is a problem to begin with.

The Effects of Anxious Attachment

Anxious attachment can affect just about every sphere of your life - often in a negative way. Without giving too much away in the first chapter, here are a few areas that are affected:

1. Romantic Relationships
Anxious attachment rears its ugly head most often in romantic relationships as the sufferer constantly seeks validation and

reassurance, or is preoccupied with their partner's time and commitment. This is where clingy and needy behavior stems from, as sufferers become overly anxious and perceive even the slightest bit of distance as abandonment. Meeting these constant, often irrational demands is not easy, and causes strain in many relationships.

2. Friendships

A friendship, too, is another type of relationship and is also subject to the effects of anxious attachment. Anxious attachment sufferers generally struggle with trust issues, often assuming that their friends, too, will abandon them at any moment. This leads to insecurity, jealousy, and a need for constant contact that does nothing more than drive friends away.

3. Work and Career

Not even the workplace is safe from the effects of anxious attachment as the sufferer constantly seeks validation from their boss and co-workers. While praise and reassurance are both great for letting an employee know they are doing a great job, those with anxious attachments seek out validation as they fear rejection or criticism. This fear leads to stress and an inability to focus on the tasks at hand.

4. Self-Esteem or Confidence

It's no secret that anxious attachment can take a toll on one's self-esteem and confidence as constant fear of abandonment or rejection can make you feel unworthy of love. It is important to remember that those with anxious attachment often internalize many of their thoughts or feelings, which can affect their self-esteem and confidence.

5. Emotional Well-Being or Mental Health

Anxious attachment has a profound impact on the emotional well-being or mental health of the sufferer. Stress, depression, chronic anxiety, and other mental health disorders are often a result of the effects of anxious attachment and should be managed carefully.

6. Parenting

Anxious attachment sufferers have it pretty hard when they become parents. Constantly questioning if they are good enough, or if they are able to properly care for their child, anxious attachment creeps in as overprotectiveness or an inability to set appropriate boundaries when it comes to parenting their children. This, in turn, has the potential to affect their child's emotional development and well-being.

7. Physical Health

Stress and anxiety are common symptoms of anxious attachment, and can have a big impact on your physical health.

Stress can lead to cardiovascular problems, a weakened immune system, and an inability to fight off disease or illness effectively.

From this, it is clear that anxious attachment has far-reaching effects on every sphere of the sufferer's life. Attachment styles can vary across cultures and societies, but can change over time based on life experiences, therapy, personal growth, and learning the tools needed to tackle the anxious attachment head-on.

Anxious Attachment: The Root Cause

Anxious attachment, also referred to as anxious-preoccupied attachment, develops from a combination of genetic, environmental, and relational factors. Simply put, it is a learned behavior that stems from experiences in early life or as the result of a trauma. And while there is no single root cause, there are several contributors that could explain the development of anxious attachment.

1. **Early Caregiver Relationships**

One of the most common factors that influence your attachment style is the quality of the relationship with your early caregiver - your parent or another primary caregiver. Anxious attachment results from inconsistent or unpredictable caregiving during infancy and childhood, and is likely caused by parents or caregivers who are emotionally unavailable or not consistently responsive, resulting in insecurity and anxiety.

2. Traumatic Experiences

Trauma, or another distressing experience, like loss, or separation from caregivers can have a big impact on anxious attachment tendencies as they create a heightened sensitivity to the potential of abandonment and a persistent fear of losing important relationships.

3. Overprotective Parenting

The complete opposite of inconsistent caregiving, overprotective parenting, too, can give rise to anxious attachment as children struggle to assert their independence or autonomy in the wake of an intrusive or controlling parent.

4. Early Experiences

Rejection, criticism, and neglect can lead to feelings of unworthiness and a belief that you constantly need to seek validation and reassurance from others. These experiences fuel the need for validation that is so common in those with anxious attachment.

5. Modeling Attachment Styles

Children often model the attachment styles that they observe in their parents or other caregivers. If a child is exposed to an anxious or avoidant attachment, they tend to internalize the patterns and replicate them in their own relationships with others.

6. Biological Factors

Genetic and neurobiological factors could have an impact on your attachment style. Variations in neurotransmitter systems, like dopamine and oxytocin have been associated with attachment behaviors. ScienceDirect.com is a great resource for materials explaining these variations and how they impact your attachment style.

7. Temperament

An individual's level of sensitivity and reactivity can shape their attachment style. Highly sensitive people are more prone to develop anxious attachments than those who are not.

Understanding the root cause of anxious attachment is both important and necessary to address and possibly reshape the attachment patterns or style to foster healthier, more secure relationships. Cognitive behavioral therapy, which we will discuss in later chapters, is a particularly effective technique that can help you with your anxious attachment, giving you the tools you need to overcome your insecurity and anxieties and help you transition towards a more secure attachment style.

Anxious Attachment Vs. Secure Attachments: The Big Difference

Attachment plays a pivotal role in shaping our experiences, our perceptions of love, and the course of our lives. Each of us carries a unique attachment style that is a blueprint for how we navigate intimacy, vulnerability and emotional connection.

Anxious attachment is a learned behavior or response that can very well be unlearned or changed. While this book focuses on overcoming anxious attachment and its many challenges, it is necessary to differentiate between an anxious or unhealthy attachment versus a secure or healthy attachment.

Knowing the effects of anxious attachment, let's now take a look at the characteristics of secure attachment styles and how they differ from your anxious attachment style.

Secure attachments have the following attributes:

1. Comfort in independence

Individuals with a secure attachment style are quite comfortable with their levels of independence, but also their intimacy in their relationships with others. They are more than self-sufficient, and are capable of self-soothing when their anxiety is trying to get the best of them.

2. Trust and confidence
Trust and confidence go hand in hand with secure attachments as individuals have the ability to trust themselves and their partners, believing in the reliability and security of their relationships.

3. Effective communication
Securely attached individuals are skilled at open and effective communication that allows them to express their needs, feelings, wants, and desires without fear of rejection or abandonment.

4. Emotional regulation
Self-regulation of one's emotions is an important aspect of a secure attachment. Individuals with a more secure attachment style have healthy coping mechanisms as opposed to those exhibited by anxious attachers. They can safely manage their own emotions without relying on their partners, friends or family to intervene and make them feel seen and heard.

5. Healthy boundaries
No relationship can survive without boundaries in place, and for those with a secure attachment style, healthy boundaries are the order of the day. These individuals are more than capable of

balancing their own needs with those of their partner, and do so while respecting their partner's boundaries as well as their own.

6. Less fear of abandonment

While no relationship is free of some degree of worrying that your partner may abandon you, securely attached individuals do not experience this fear, insecurity or doubt as often or intensely as those with an anxious attachment style. They are able to regulate their emotions and change their negative thought patterns by themselves, restoring calm and order to their thought processes.

It is important to note again that attachment styles are not fixed and can change at any time with self-awareness, personal growth, and therapy. Those with anxious attachment need to be dedicated to working towards becoming more securely attached by first accepting that there is a problem, addressing their fears, and committing to change their attachment style.

This is just the beginning of your journey, so be sure to carry on to chapter two to find out more about anxious attachment and how it can affect every part of your life.

Chapter Two: A Deep Dive into Anxious Attachment

◊

In this chapter, we'll do a deep dive into exactly what anxious attachment is, look at the signs or diagnosis criteria, and also look at ways it can manifest itself in your romantic relationships.

Let's uncover why some individuals seem to navigate the waters of love, trust, and emotional connection effortlessly while others find themselves caught up in a whirlwind of doubt, insecurity and longing.

Anxious Attachment: A Life Sentence or a Changeable Diagnosis?

Now that we know what anxious attachment is, and that it likely stems from how your needs were met, or not met, as a child, we need to analyze how it manifests itself in your romantic relationships and if there is a way to heal and change your behaviors.

Anxious attachment is not a life sentence, but rather a changeable pattern that can be transformed with self-awareness, personal growth, and, of course, the support of your partner, loved ones, and friends. Attachment styles are not fixed or permanent. They are learned patterns of relating to others and can evolve and change over time.

Here are a few points to consider regarding how to change your attachment style and form more secure attachments that lead to healthier relationships and an increase in your overall well-being:

Awareness

Recognizing that you have an anxious attachment style is the first step towards change. Self-awareness allows you to understand how your attachment patterns impact your relationships and emotional well-being.

Therapy and Intervention

Therapies, like cognitive behavioral therapy, can be effective in helping those with anxious attachment develop more secure attachment patterns. CBT is one of the more effective tools you can use to overcome your anxious attachment.

Self-Help and Self-Work

Self-help practices are a great and effective method of addressing your attachment style. Books, practicing mindfulness and emotional regulation, and engaging in exercises to challenge and reframe the negative thought patterns brought about by anxious attachment are all key to changing your attachment style.

Personal growth and self-development can contribute to changes in attachment style. As you work on improving your self-esteem, self-worth, and self-compassion, you will become less dependent on external validation and feel more secure within yourself.

Healthy Relationships

Healthy, secure, and supportive relationships play a pivotal role in changing your attachment style and saying goodbye to negative thought patterns. Positive relationships provide opportunities for healing, growth, and the development of a secure attachment.

Consistency and Time

Changing attachment patterns takes time and consistent effort. Prepare yourself for setbacks and challenges along the way, but never give up. Persevere and see the significant progress you are making in changing your attachment style.

Flexibility

It is critically important to remember that your attachment style is fluid. And while you may display an anxious attachment style in your romantic relationship, you might display a different one in another situation or relationship with, say, your friends. This flexibility demonstrates that change is, in fact, possible, and that you are not defined by your anxious attachment style.

Embracing Self-Compassion

Practicing self-compassion, or self-love as it is more commonly referred to, is crucial on your journey to change your anxious attachment style to a more secure attachment style. Self-acceptance, patience, and forgiving yourself are all essential components of personal growth and transformation.

Anxious Attachment and Your Romantic Relationships

In the vast landscape of human emotions, romantic relationships stand as one of the most profound and captivating experiences that we can embark on. When they are good, they can be a source of joy, companionship, and personal growth. But, for someone with an anxious attachment, the path to this love can be littered with uncertainty, insecurity, and a craving for reassurance.

There are a number of unique challenges and opportunities that arise when anxious attachers are in a romantic relationship. And while these may seem more like hurdles that stand in the way of your happiness, they can, too, help you overcome the attachment style that appears to do nothing more than leave you stressed, anxious, and frustrated.

Someone once referred to a relationship as both the poison and the cure for anxious attachment. Sounds a bit ridiculous, right? How can a relationship be both good and bad for someone who suffers from anxious attachment?

Relationships: The Poison for Anxious Attachment

Have you ever been in a relationship with someone who is extremely needy or clingy? Did they, too, require constant validation and reassurance that you loved them and that you wouldn't abandon them? This is what it is like for those who suffer from anxious attachment - the constant fear that they are not good enough and that their partner will leave them at the drop of a hat.

This thinking is the poison that we referred to, and leads to the anxious attacher acting in an extreme manner in response to any perceived threats. A good example of this is when the anxious attachment partner pushes for more intimacy or is even more clingy than usual, often resulting in their partner pulling away as they feel stifled and that they need to get away from this behavior.

The negative aspects of a relationship for an anxious attachment sufferer can manifest in the following ways:

1. **Heightened Anxiety:** Relationships tend to heighten an anxious individual's need for reassurance to overcome their feelings of abandonment and other behaviors that lead to chronic stress and emotional turmoil.

2. **Dependency:** Anxious attachment often leads to emotional dependency on a partner, which in turn not only places strain on the relationship, but also hampers the anxious attacher's personal growth and independence.

3. **Conflict and Tension:** Anxious attachment leads to frequent conflicts in relationships. The constant need for reassurance, coupled with the anxiety surrounding the fear of abandonment, can create tension and misunderstanding for both partners.

4. **Impact on Your Partner:** The demands of an anxious attachment style can be challenging for the partner, as they feel overwhelmed by the constant need for validation and they struggle to meet the emotional needs of their anxiously attached loved one.

The Cure

Looking at the above scenario, it is hard to imagine that there is any solution at all to the clinginess or extreme behavior that an anxious attachment partner would exhibit. But as we have mentioned before, a relationship is quite possibly the cure, too, as the sufferer will feel calm and secure in their partner's company or presence.

See what we mean when we say that a relationship is both the poison and the cure?

It seems that no matter what happens, or how hard you work at a relationship, those with anxious attachments are often their own worst enemy as they struggle to control their emotions and inevitably jeopardize their own relationships.

Here is a breakdown of just how a relationship can help someone deal with the complexities of their anxious attachment:

1. **Emotional Fulfillment:** A relationship can provide a sense of security or fulfillment for someone with an anxious attachment as the presence of a loving partner can soothe their anxieties and provide reassurance that they are loved, valued, and cared for.

2. **Increased Self-Esteem:** A loving and supportive partner can boost the self-esteem and self-worth of those with anxious attachment. Knowing they are loved and cherished can counteract the feelings of inadequacy that they so often feel as a result of their attachment style.

3. **Growth and Healing:** A healthy relationship often serves as a catalyst for personal growth and healing through the support of a loving partner that helps an anxious attacher learn to address and overcome their attachment issues.

4. **Positivity:** A good and happy relationship can offer more than just companionship as it brings joy and shared experiences, too. These positive moments can provide a sense of happiness and belonging.

Anxious Attachment in a Relationship

Now that we have looked at how relationships can be both a poison and a cure for someone with anxious attachment, let's move on to a few of the more classic signs that could indicate that you have an anxious attachment style.

We touched on these very briefly in chapter one, but now we'll look at what those who suffer from anxious attachment go through on a daily basis as they navigate the slippery slopes of their relationships.

Identifying and acknowledging that you might have an anxious attachment style is the first step to getting help, so this is the time when I urge you to be brutally honest as you go through these signs and symptoms of anxious attachment.

#1: You are highly attuned to your partner's needs and continuously put them first, often prioritizing their needs over your own.

Before you jump up and down and say that this is how relationships are supposed to be, let us clarify that there is nothing wrong with putting your partner's needs first. It is when you completely ignore or forget about your own needs that the problem comes in. Your needs should never be pushed aside in favor of those of your partners. Self-love is important in a relationship, and so, too, is allowing your partner to make their own decisions and do what makes them happy.

#2: You constantly seek validation or reassurance that you are worthy of love and that your partner does, in fact, love you.

We all want the comfort of knowing that we are loved, right? So how can seeking validation be a bad thing? Here's how: when the seeking of this validation borders on obsessive, almost clingy, behavior that drives a wedge between you and your partner. Does your partner regularly tell you that they love you? Yes? If you are still questioning if they do, you could have an anxious attachment.

#3: You fear rejection and abandonment.
This relates to all spheres of your life, and not necessarily just your romantic relationships. Fear of rejection and abandonment by your partner, friends, family members, and even your boss or co-workers could signal an anxious attachment.

#4: You constantly worry that things will go wrong in your relationship.
It's normal to worry that your relationship is not going the way you want it to. And yes, we could all stand to work on our relationships a bit more. But what about when things are good, and your relationship is actually in a good place? Do you still have that overwhelming feeling of anxiety that it is all going to come crashing down at any moment and you'll be left alone and brokenhearted?

#5: You get jealous or suspicious of your partner's behavior or actions.
Again, it is normal to feel those little pangs of jealousy when your partner does something you are not too happy about. But, when that jealousy or suspicion arises over even the smallest

action, there might be a bigger issue at hand - and that issue is your anxious attachment. If you are constantly finding fault with or suspecting that your partner is going to suddenly up and leave, you likely have an anxious attachment.

#6: You are emotionally reactive.
Do you find yourself struggling to control your emotions? Are you emotionally reactive to even the slightest upset? Yes, there could be many other reasons for your emotional state, but if you are reading this, you already know what the problem is. Those who suffer from anxious attachment often become agitated or overly emotional when faced with any relationship issue.

#7: You over-analyze everything.
Over-analyzing every aspect of your relationship, including reading into texts and going over conversations in your head repeatedly is another sign that you could have an anxious attachment. Individuals who suffer from anxious attachment often look for a hidden or deeper meaning in every text, email, conversation, or interaction with their partner, friends, and family members, creating a problem where there is none.

Have you agreed to any or all of the statements above? Are you in a relationship with someone who displays some, or all of the traits we have identified? Suffering from or loving someone with an anxious attachment style is by no means easy. Change is possible, and so, too, is healing, but this takes time and more than a little patience.

Loving Someone with Anxious Attachment

Anxious attachment comes from a place of deep-seated fears, an overwhelming need for reassurance, and a longing for closeness and intimacy. Living with an anxious attachment style is not easy, and for those whose partners suffer from this, the battle is far from over as they have to adapt the way they deal with the various issues that may arise.

It is important to understand that your partner with anxious attachment feels unworthy of love, and that they fear abandonment. From random bursts of anger to internalizing their negative feelings and all but shutting down, there are a range of emotions that you may need to deal with.

Anxious individuals are warm, affectionate, and deeply caring, and their magnetic pull can be incredibly enticing. When they love, they do so with an intensity that can be both captivating and reassuring, as they are attuned to their partner's emotional needs. Consistent presence, words of affirmation, and non-judgmental support are like a lifeline for someone with anxious attachment, as they need to hear that they are loved, that their partner will not abandon them, and that their feelings are valid.

Clingy behavior and insecurity are often the order of the day for those with anxious attachment, and it is crucial to address these behaviors with patience and empathy. Rather than pushing them away, gently communicating the need for space and time - while reassuring them of love and commitment - is important.

Here are a few tips on how to take control of the situation and help your partner with anxious attachment feel more secure in your relationship:

Tip #1: Listen

This sounds fairly easy, right? You, as their partner, need to create a safe space for them to vent their emotions, share their concerns, and also help you understand just what it is that they are feeling.

Your job is to offer your unwavering support, validating their feelings while challenging their insecurities and fears. You can make a difference by committing to open and honest communication that encourages and embraces their fears and anxieties.

Tip #2: Encourage Self-Help Therapies and Techniques

There is no shame in admitting that the help you are able to offer is limited. And in extreme cases, even your reassurance might not be enough. Encourage your partner to seek help in the form of self-help guides, and do a little research on therapy techniques that have been known to help those with anxious attachment.

Tip #3: Establish Clear Boundaries

Neurotic behavior often goes hand in hand with anxious attachment, and you might just find your partner scrutinizing your every move or questioning your every action. Set clear boundaries regarding their behavior, and let them know that you are there for them but won't tolerate certain things. Work together to define what is both comfortable and respectful for each of you within the relationship.

Be loving and open in your discussion on boundaries, and reinforce the idea that you are there to stay and that you want to help them.

Tip #4: Be Consistent

Consistency is key when dealing with a loved one who has an anxious attachment. Be consistent in your approach to helping them, and help them feel more secure. If you know that certain behaviors are a trigger, try your best to curb these actions and focus on enforcing that they are important and loved.

Having someone to lean on for support and comfort while facing the challenges that anxious attachment can bring is so important. And while you might be hopeful that this support will come from your partner, it might not always happen. Find support from those who are able and willing to help you overcome your anxious attachment. Turn to your friends and family on the hard days, and let them love and support you like you need to be supported, while going through the tips and strategies that this book will identify.

Tip #5: Navigating a Rollercoaster of Emotions

Be prepared for the occasional emotional turbulence. Anxious individuals can experience intense highs and lows. Patience and understanding during these moments can make all the difference and help your partner feel that you are there for them and that you want to help them navigate these emotions.

Much of this emotional turmoil can be resolved by consistently demonstrating your commitment, providing reassurance, and fostering open communication that helps your partner feel more secure within the relationship.

Anxious Attachment: A Lesson for All

As we bring this chapter to a close, we want to reinforce the fact that anxious attachment can be healed. Loving someone with anxious attachment might not be easy, but you can make a difference to how they respond to certain situations and actions. It is a journey of empathy, patience, and personal growth for both partners. Understanding their anxieties, providing unwavering support, and nurturing the relationship will create a love that is secure, fulfilling, and built on a foundation of trust and understanding.

Anxious attachment holds a mirror to our shared vulnerabilities and desires and reminds us that, at our core, we all seek love, security, and understanding. For those who battle with an anxious attachment style, these vulnerabilities and desires are cast into the limelight more often than most, leaving the anxious attacher craving reassurance and validation.

In this chapter, we have learnt that the yearning for reassurance, the fear of abandonment, and the constant battle for connection are universal experiences that touch us all. And while it may affect some more than others, there will be times when we are both the bearer and recipient of these emotions.

Identifying and acknowledging that there is a problem is the first step in a long journey to healing, so take note of the signs and symptoms we identified in this chapter. Take a long hard look at your behavior and how you react to certain situations, and be honest in acknowledging that there is something wrong. Know that it is not your fault, and likely stems from childhood trauma or some other issue that might require therapy to heal.

Love is a force that drives us to seek connection, overcome our fears, and heal our wounds. It is, essentially, a testament to our shared humanity, resilience, and capacity for change as we seek to transform our anxious attachment into a source of strength and wisdom. This is only the beginning, and it is important to remember that the best is yet to come.

Chapter Three: Anxious Attachment and Your Relationship

✠

Chapter three is going to be a bit different as we focus on the effects of anxious attachment and your relationship with your partner. With intimacy being a necessity in a relationship, it is important to understand that those with anxious attachment crave this intimacy more than others. And while you might not think this is necessarily a bad thing, it might drive your partner away rather than draw them closer to you because they feel smothered.

I know - it all sounds pretty confusing. How can too much intimacy be a bad thing? Let's get straight into the issue of anxious attachment and relationships as we analyze just how this attachment style can affect your relationship with your romantic partner by looking at:

- The effects of anxious attachment on your romantic relationship
- Men vs. women: How anxious attachment affects both genders
- Tips and tricks to change your behavior

The Effects of Anxious Attachment on Your Relationship

An anxious attachment style can wreak havoc on your romantic relationships and your partner. Your fear of abandonment, overwhelming need for intimacy, and constant search for validation have the opposite effect that you think it will, and might just push your partner away.

Understanding the many challenges of your anxious attachment is key to changing your attachment style and learning to form secure attachments with your partner.

Here are a few of the more common effects that anxious attachment could have on your relationship:

A Need for Reassurance
Anxious partners seek constant reassurance from their partners to quash those fears of abandonment or rejection. This, in turn, leads to emotionally draining conversations that see your partner repeating themselves constantly in their quest to get through to you that they won't suddenly up and leave and that you are, in fact, good enough and worthy of the love you so desperately crave.

Because anxious attachment has its roots in childhood, adult anxious attachment sufferers have a deep-seated fear of losing their partner or other attachment figures. This, in turn, leads to insecurity, anxiety, low self-esteem, negative thought patterns, and a fear of abandonment.

It is important to understand that the need for reassurance for those with anxious attachment is not a sign of weakness or inadequacy, but rather a reflection of their attachment style. Frequent calls, texts, and requests for reassurance may become overwhelming for the partner, but is a coping mechanism for someone with an anxious attachment.

Insecurity and Jealousy
Anxious attachment sufferers are more prone to feelings of intense insecurity and jealousy that more often than not lead to unnecessary conflict and tension in the relationship. While you may feel that keeping tabs on your partner's every move is a way for you to feel secure, it can quickly have the opposite effect and drive your partner away.

Insecurity and jealousy are often present due to the core fears and emotions associated with anxious attachment. The core fears are:

- A fear of abandonment

- Low self-esteem
- Negative thought patterns
- Need for reassurance
- Difficulty trusting others

These feelings of insecurity and jealousy are not the flaws of the anxious attachment sufferer, but rather in their attachment style and past experiences. Addressing these feelings is key to developing healthier coping mechanisms and strategies.

Fear of Abandonment
This is one of the biggest effects of an anxious attachment style on your relationship. Yes, you are battling with insecurities and fears that your partner could leave you because you are not good enough, but what you need to understand is that this fear of abandonment and rejection may only push your partner further away. Fear of abandonment often leads to clinginess and neurotic behavior that can rear its ugly head at any time - often without cause or reason.

Anxious attachment stems from childhood experiences or some other trauma. This creates a sense of unpredictability and insecurity in all relationships and makes the sufferer more aware of or hypervigilant to signs of abandonment. Inconsistent caregiving, negative thought patterns, and a fear of rejection go hand in hand with an anxious attachment style, and need to be addressed to help the sufferer form more secure attachments and have healthier relationships with their partner and with others.

Overanalyzing EVERYTHING

Overanalyzing your partner's actions, words, and behavior is your way of looking for signs that they may abandon you. This can create unnecessary stress on you and also on your relationship. Yes, it is easy enough to say "Stop overthinking and overanalyzing everything", but I know that it is not as simple as that.

Recognizing this and working on healthier communication are critical to reducing overthinking, relationship strain, and building a more secure and trusting relationship.

Difficulty Trusting Your Partner

Trust issues are fairly common in all relationships, but none more so than a relationship burdened with an anxious attachment. A constant need for validation and a heightened sensitivity to perceived threats only fuel this mistrust and can lead to a fair amount of arguments.

Trust issues often arise due to the following:

- Fear of abandonment

- The constant need for reassurance
- Overanalyzing your partner's behaviors
- Clinginess and insecurity
- Self-doubt
- Anticipating and presuming rejection
- Past relationship trauma
- Lack of self-soothing skills

It is important to note that these trust issues are not a reflection of your partner's behavior, but are rooted in your anxious attachment style and past experiences. Overcoming trust issues is possible, and involves a combination of self-awareness, open communication, and self-soothing techniques. You can work with your partner to build trust over time and create a healthier, and more secure relationship.

Push-Pull Dynamics

A push-pull dynamic is never a good thing for any relationship. This dynamic exists when the anxious attachment sufferer alternates between craving intimacy and closeness and completely pulling away. Often a coping mechanism to protect themselves from the perceived hurt of being abandoned, a push-pull dynamic can cause much confusion and frustration for your partner.

The push-pull dynamic can be challenging for both the anxious attacher and their partner, and can lead to conflicts, misunderstandings, and emotional exhaustion. Breaking the patterns of a push-pull dynamic is possible, and requires self-awareness, open communication, and sometimes therapy in extreme cases.

A Lack of Boundaries

Boundaries are an integral and important part of every relationship, but in a relationship marred by anxious attachment, these boundaries are often unhealthy and lead to codependency. Clear boundaries are the only remedy for this effect of anxious attachment, but that, too, is easier said than done.

Individuals with anxious attachment generally have a lack of boundaries stemming from their underlying fears and insecurities. Developing healthy communication and boundary-setting skills is vital to overcome this.

Communication Challenges

No relationship can survive without clear and regular communication. This effective communication is not always possible for those with anxious attachment, as anxiety, fear of abandonment, and a lack of trust make it quite a challenge to express their needs and concerns calmly and clearly.

A constant need for reassurance coupled with overanalyzing and misinterpreting what your partner says can lead to communication issues. Addressing these communication challenges requires self-awareness, open and honest conversations with your partner, and a form of therapy or self-help tool that will help you work through underlying attachment-related fears and anxieties.

The Impact on Your Partner

This next effect is an important one as it talks about how your need for constant reassurance and validation can be emotionally taxing for your partner. Yes, dealing with your anxious attachment and its many issues is not easy, but it can lead to feelings of suffocation and frustration in your partner.

Partners of those with anxious attachment can experience a range of challenges in the relationship due to the dynamics of this attachment style. These may vary depending on the coping mechanisms, communication skills, and degree of anxious attachment.

Common challenges include:

- Stress and emotional drain
- Feelings of responsibility

- A feeling of walking on eggshells
- Frustration and burnout
- Difficulty with boundaries
- A misinterpretation of intentions
- Feeling overwhelmed

Negativity

If you're constantly anxious or fearful that your partner will abandon you, you are creating a cycle of negativity within your relationship. Conflict and emotional turmoil are just two of the side effects of this cycle of negativity, but they are treatable. Start by following the tips we'll be outlining a little later in this chapter.

These effects can vary in intensity, and while you may experience some, you might not experience them all. If your relationship sees only a few of these manifesting themselves, you can pat yourself on the back for choosing a sensitive partner who is committed to helping you deal with your anxious attachment style. But, if you can tick every box and have noticed that all these effects are present in your relationship, there is some work to be done.

Recognizing that there is a problem is the first and most crucial step in addressing the challenges that come with anxious attachment and your relationship with your partner. The question is: Are you ready to put in the effort and work that it takes to overcome the effects of your anxious attachment on your relationship?

Men Vs. Women: Anxious Attachment and the Sexes

Anxious attachment can rear its ugly head in different ways for men and women. And while it should be dealt with in the same way - by working on and changing the behaviors that could ultimately drive your partner away - there is a stark difference between how anxious attachment affects both men and women.

To get a better idea of just what these differences are, let's now look at the most common "signs" of anxious attachment and how they relate to each gender.

Expressing Emotions

It's no secret that women are more likely to express their emotions more often and more openly. Thanks to societal norms and what is culturally acceptable, men are more likely to suppress or hide their feelings of anxiety or fear. This often leads to them bottling up their emotions and internalizing their feelings. Men who have anxious attachment find it challenging to initiate emotional conversation, and will need more prompting to share their feelings.

Women, on the other hand, have the freedom to express their emotions openly, and is why anxious attachment is often seen more as a woman's problem rather than something that affects both genders equally.

Coping Mechanisms

This is an interesting one, as women are the ones who are more likely to seek that all-important reassurance from their partner when their anxiety is at an all-time high and they fear abandonment. Men, however, are far more likely to withdraw from a situation or adopt avoidant behaviors that see them internalizing their fears and anxiety.

Again, this is largely due to societal and gender norms that dictate what is acceptable behavior for men and women, and is a big problem for those who suffer from anxious attachment in their relationships.

Relationship Dynamics and Gender Roles

Anxious attachment creates a power dynamic within a relationship. Whether you agree with this statement or not, it is a fact that men are generally seen as the protectors or the "strong" ones in any relationship. Women, on the other hand, are usually seen as the emotional ones who have no trouble expressing their emotions and can do so freely.

This vulnerability can lead to a breakdown in communication as men with anxious attachment feel that they need to "get over it" and that they are not able to express their fears and anxieties without judgment.

Getting Help

Did you know that men are far less likely to seek therapy or support for their anxious attachment than women do? There is an ugly stigma that only weak men seek mental health support, leading to many men suffering in silence and being unable to deal with their problems openly.

Watch any Hollywood movie and nine times out of ten the "heroine" is in some form of therapy to deal with her emotional and mental issues. Society has created this perception, and it is up to you to shatter this perception and make it clear that getting help is not only brave but necessary to deal with anxious attachment and its many effects.

Anxious attachment is by no means a gendered issue, and can affect both men and women equally. Understanding the "gender norms" that unfortunately exist is just one way in which you can deal with anxious attachment and its effects on your relationships. Self-awareness, effective communication, and the willingness to work together to combat anxious attachment can help build a secure and fulfilling relationship for you and your partner.

Understanding your Anxious Attachment

As we already pointed out, understanding and acknowledging your anxious attachment is crucial for many reasons. And while it may seem like an enormous task, it can be done and you can overcome your anxious attachment and have a healthy, loving relationship with your partner.

Here are the benefits that await you when you put in the effort and truly acknowledge and understand your anxious attachment style and the effects it has on your relationship with your partner:

#1: Self-Awareness
Recognizing and understanding your anxious attachment style is the very first step toward greater self-awareness. It allows you to understand why you react the way you do, but also what triggers you. This awareness will help you gain insight into your emotions, thoughts, and behaviors, and will lead to personal growth and self-improvement.

#2: Improved Relationships
Understanding your attachment style is instrumental in building healthier and more fulfilling relationships. When you are fully

aware of your anxious tendencies, you can work to manage them more effectively. This means communicating your needs more clearly, setting appropriate boundaries, and addressing those insecurities and fears that may crop up from time to time. Communication is key for better understanding and connection between you and your partner.

#3: Breaking the Cycle

Anxious attachment stems from early life experiences or patterns of behavior you developed during childhood. By acknowledging your anxious attachment style, you can break the cycle of unhealthy relationship dynamics that have plagued you. Recognizing that your attachment style is not a fixed trait allows you to work on changing it and creating more positive relationship experiences.

#4: Personal Growth

Acknowledging your anxious attachment style is an incredible empowering process that encourages personal growth as you confront and address your insecurities and anxieties. This is a journey of self-discovery that can lead to increased self-esteem, self-confidence, and emotional resilience.

#5: Emotional Regulation

Understanding your attachment style will equip you with the tools to better manage your emotions. You can learn to recognize and regulate your anxiety and insecurity, resulting in an increase in emotional control and a reduction of emotional turbulence that would positively affect both you and your relationships.

#6: Empathy and Compassion
Self-awareness of your anxious attachment style will foster empathy and compassion towards yourself and others. Recognizing the fact that attachment styles are formed in response to past experiences and that they are not a reflection of your worth as a person can help you be more understanding and empathetic to both yourself and your partner.

Tips and Tricks to Change Your Behavior

Relationships are like a journey and come with many emotions, expectations and, yes, vulnerabilities that need to be addressed to build a better bond with your partner. Without going into too much detail, I want to provide a few helpful tips on how you can manage your anxious attachment and have a happy, secure relationship with your partner.

Remember when we said that communication is key to the survival of any relationship? Well, this is the focus of my tips as I guide you in how to talk to your partner about your insecurities and fears as you tackle your anxious attachment head-on.

Let's get started.

Tip #1: Understanding and Acknowledging Your Anxious Attachment

The first step in this important journey is to understand and acknowledge your anxious attachment. Take some time to understand the root cause of your anxious attachment and how this affects your attachment style.

Self-awareness allows you to understand why you react the way you do in relationships and may bring to light why certain patterns of behavior persist. It also helps you gain insight into your emotions, thoughts, and behaviors, which facilitate personal growth and self-improvement.

Identify what triggers your anxiety and how anxious attachment manifests itself in your current relationship and then ready yourself for a serious talk with your partner. Self-awareness can help you not only initiate the conversation but also guide you when it comes to expressing your needs clearly.

Tip #2: Choose the Right Time and Place

Bombarding your partner with a heavy topic like anxious attachment the moment they walk in the door after a long day at work is not a good idea. Choose a time when you are both free and able to have a discussion where you won't be interrupted or distracted, and make sure to choose a comfortable spot. A relaxed partner is a receptive partner, so choose your time wisely.

Tip #3: Be as Open and Honest as Possible
This is not the time to hide what you are feeling in fear of judgment or that you'll scare your partner away. Be open and honest as you communicate your needs, triggers, anxiety, and what it is that you want from the discussion.

Avoid sounding overly critical or accusatory by keeping the focus on yourself and referring to your issues with your anxious attachment and how they affect your perceptions and needs within the relationship. Do not under any circumstances blame your partner for your anxious attachment. It is not their fault, and you should focus on reassuring them that you are not blaming them, but rather asking for their assistance in dealing with it.

Tip #4: Identify Your Triggers
Anxiety is an awful thing to live with. Whether you are anxious about your fears of abandonment or feeling that you are not worthy of love, be honest with your partner and explain what it is that triggers your anxieties. Again, do not blame them or state what they are doing wrong but rather tell them what you need to feel secure and comfortable in your relationship.

Help them help you by providing them with examples of what they can do to make you feel secure and less anxious.

Tip #5: Communicate, Communicate, Communicate
You get the gist of where this one is going. Communicate your emotional needs with your partner in a clear and calm manner. If you need a bit more reassurance than they are currently giving you, tell them. Communication is the key to overcoming or managing your anxious attachment, so use it to your advantage and express your feelings and needs clearly.

Tip #6: Listen
This might seem like a strange tip, but it is an important one, as I urge you to listen to what your partner has to say. Once you have shared your anxieties, needs, and emotions give them a chance to have their say. Listen without becoming defensive, and understand that they are only trying to help you and not criticize or blame you for having an anxious attachment issue.

Let them ask questions and answer these to the best of your ability as they try to understand what they can do to help you manage your anxious attachment without letting it affect the relationship and ultimately drive them away.

Tip #7: DO NOT BLAME
It is so easy to blame someone else for your problems, right? This is a big no-no when you are seeking help for your anxious attachment. Focus on solving the problem together rather than playing the blame game, and have a discussion rather than an argument that sees you blaming each other rather than coming up with solutions.

Tip #8: Come up with Solutions Together
Let your partner know that you want to change your behavior by asking them to help you come up with a few solutions on how to keep your anxieties at bay and alleviate your fears of abandonment. This is not the time to feel that you are being targeted or that they are being harsh in their solutions, but rather to focus on the end goal - having a happy and secure relationship while working on your anxious attachment.

Talking to your partner can be pretty daunting, but it is essential if you really want to overcome your anxious attachment and ultimately have a secure and fulfilling relationship. Focus on honest and open communication and commit to working together to create an even stronger bond that is based on patience, trust, and support.

You can be happy and feel secure in your relationship despite your anxious attachment. You just need to want to work on it and find that common ground with your partner. Your fears and anxieties need not define you or rule your relationship. Work together and you, too, can overcome the challenges that anxious attachment brings to your relationship.

Final Thoughts

As we end this chapter, we want to reiterate that your anxious attachment is not your fault, but rather the result of not having your emotional needs properly met in your younger years. It can also be a result of trauma that you sustained from a significant event, or even a previous relationship that saw you questioning and second-guessing your every action.

Yes, anxious attachment affects those around you, but not as much as it does you. You can change. You can do better. And you can heal from this challenging attachment style and learn to form secure attachments again. It will take time. And a lot of hard work. But, at the end of the day, it is worth it!

As we journey on through the rest of the book, we'll take a look at a few great treatment options and solutions that have revolutionized the lives of those who suffer from anxious attachment. From cognitive behavioral therapy to schema therapy and affirmations, there are plenty of solutions to helping you overcome anxious attachment - you just need to find the one that works for you.

Chapter Four: Defining Boundaries and Independence

No relationship comes without hard work. And for those with anxious attachment, a healthy relationship requires overcoming the challenges that play a significant role in shaping how they navigate relationships.

Anxious attachment, too, affects the type of relationships that individuals will enter into. While you may think that anxious attachers would seek out relationships with someone with a more secure attachment style, the opposite is in fact true.

Relationship Types of Anxious Attachers

Here are the relationship types that someone with anxious attachment might find themselves in:

On-Again/Off-Again Relationships
Anxious attachers may find themselves in relationships that are characterized by frequent breakups and reunions. The fear of abandonment is quite often the driving force behind the pursuit of a partner who is emotionally unavailable or inconsistent in their commitment. This, unfortunately, can lead to a

rollercoaster of emotions and a pattern of seeking constant reassurance.

Codependent Relationships

Those with anxious attachment may be drawn to codependent relationships where their sense of self-worth is closely tied to their partner's approval and validation. In this type of relationship, the anxious attacher may sacrifice their own needs and boundaries simply to maintain the connection.

An individual with anxious attachment may also seek validation and affirmation from more than one source. This includes friends, family, and, of course, romantic partners. Their self-esteem can heavily depend on external validation, making them vulnerable to manipulation or emotional turmoil in their relationships.

One-Sided Relationships

Anxious attachers might enter into relationships where they invest a lot of emotional energy and effort into the relationship while receiving little in return. This can lead to feelings of frustration and imbalance as the anxious attacher seeks reciprocity from their significant other.

Unhealthy Attachments to Avoidant Partners

Ironically, anxious attachers are more likely to be attracted to avoidant partners who are emotionally distant or hesitant to commit to the relationship. They may see these partners as a challenge, or believe that they are able to change them, hoping to finally gain the consistent love and attention they desire.

Why?

The biggest question that many anxious attachers have is "Why?" Why do anxious attachers pursue partners that are either emotionally unavailable or completely avoidant?

Understanding the reasons behind this "phenomenon" as it were, can shed some light on this pattern of behavior. Here's what we have uncovered:

1. **Familiarity:** For anxious attachers, the inconsistency and unpredictability of a relationship with someone who has an avoidant attachment style can feel familiar, or even comforting - even when this is not healthy. People are naturally drawn to what is familiar to them, and the uncertainty of this type of relationship might mimic the emotional rollercoaster that they experienced in childhood.

2. **Complementary Needs:** Those with anxious attachment will seek closeness, validation, and

reassurance in their relationships. On the other end of the scale, avoidant attachers tend to value their independence and find it uncomfortable to get too emotionally close to someone. Contrasting needs create an attraction, as anxious attachers might find the aloofness or independence of their avoidant partners intriguing while avoidant individuals may appreciate the attention and warmth of anxious partners.

3. **Validation of Self-Worth:** Anxious attachers have low self-esteem and seek external validation to feel worthy and loved. Pursuing a partner who is emotionally unstable or inconsistent can be a way to prove their own worth. They often believe that if they can win over a partner who is hard to please, it may just validate their own desirability.

4. **A "Rescue" Fantasy:** Some individuals with anxious attachment have a subconscious desire to rescue or fix their partners, believing that helping their partner become more stable or committed will result in them receiving the consistent love and attention they so badly crave. This, in turn, leads to a pattern of trying to change or save their partner which can be emotionally draining.

5. **Drama or Intensity:** Anxious attachers may become addicted to the drama or intensity of relationships with unstable partners. The highs and lows of this relationship can be emotionally charged and addictive, even if it is not emotionally satisfying or healthy in the long run.

6. **Lack of Self-Awareness:** It is difficult for people to fully understand their attachment style and how it can influence or impact their relationship choices. Anxious individuals might find themselves repeatedly attracted to emotionally unstable partners without understanding why.

7. **Healing Past Wounds:** Some people enter into relationships with anxious or avoidant partners with the hopes of healing their own attachment wounds. Anxious attachers believe that if they can change their partner's behaviors, they will make them more emotionally available. Avoidant individuals, however, hope to become more comfortable with intimacy through relationships with their anxious partner. This dynamic sadly leads to frustration and unhappiness as anxious attachers feel that their partner's emotional availability is a form of rejection. Understanding that this is just a "symptom" of the avoidant partner's attachment style is key.

8. **A Repetition of Patterns**: People often unconsciously repeat patterns from their part in their adult relationships. Anxious attachers may be used to chasing after emotionally distant partners due to their childhood experiences, while avoidant attachers are more accustomed to distancing themselves when someone gets too close. These patterns lead to the push-pull dynamic in relationships that we covered in a previous chapter.

Attachment styles, whether anxious or avoidant, create challenges in relationships. However it is important to remember that your attachment style is not set in stone and that you need to work on understanding or modifying your attachment patterns to build healthier, more satisfying relationships.

Dependent Vs. Independent: A Peek into an Anxious Attacher's Mind

There is a very thin line between dependence and independence for anxious attachers. This creates a tension between the need for emotional closeness and the desire for independence which manifests itself in several ways. From an overreliance on partners to a difficulty with boundaries, there are a few key aspects of anxious attachment that could affect an individual's dependence or independence in a relationship.

Let's look at these aspects in more detail as we try to understand why these patterns exist, and what anxious attachers should do to create a healthier balance between their need for closeness and their independence.

Overreliance on a Partner

Overreliance by an anxious attacher can lead to many challenges in relationships, including feelings of suffocation, emotional exhaustion, and relationship strain. Anxious attachers may struggle to maintain their independence because they are highly dependent on their partner for emotional security. They are hesitant to make decisions or pursue personal interests without their partner's input or presence.

Neglecting Personal Needs

Anxious attachers sometimes neglect their own needs or interests in the pursuit of maintaining their relationship. They will prioritize their partner's needs, wishes, and desires over their own, leading to a sense of imbalance. A lack of assertiveness may also be a factor as anxious attachers may find it difficult to express their own needs clearly and directly. You should also be aware of the guilt and obligation that anxious attachers often feel as they prioritize their partner's needs above their own as they feel they are responsible for their partner's happiness and well-being. Self-neglect is a very real and very common way of life for many anxious attachers.

Constant Reassurance-Seeking

Anxious attachers may engage in constant reassurance-seeking behaviors like checking in with their partner repeatedly, or seeking validation for their actions. This is often done as a way to manage their anxiety but could actually hinder their ability to be more self-reliant and independent.

A desire for emotional connection is quite often the reason behind their need for constant reassurance as they aim to maintain a constant emotional bond with their partner. Reassurance-seeking is, however, a natural behavior that many individuals display, and this is not always connected to their attachment style but more to a person's need to be loved and validated.

Difficulty with Boundaries

Establishing and maintaining personal boundaries can be challenging for those with an anxious attachment style. These individuals may have trouble asserting their independence when necessary, and may struggle with setting limits within their relationships. This often gives rise to insecurities and challenges that see the anxious attacher having difficulty with establishing and maintaining healthy boundaries.

It's no secret that an anxious attacher tends to be more of a people-pleaser than those with other attachment styles, as they prioritize their partner's wishes and needs over their own to seek validation and approval. Prioritizing another person's needs over your own can lead to a reluctance to assert boundaries that could upset or inconvenience your partner.

Anxious attachers have just as much difficulty respecting boundaries as they do setting them, and could react negatively to any boundaries that they perceive as possible threats to the relationship. By actively working on boundary-setting, individuals with anxious attachment can create healthier, more balanced relationships that respect both their own needs and the needs of their partners.

Achieving a healthy balance between dependence and independence in relationships can be quite challenging for those with anxious attachment, but it is not an impossible endeavor. Striking the right balance is crucial, and will go a long way in fostering fulfilling and secure relationships.

Here are a few more ways in which an anxious attacher can learn to find the all-important equilibrium between dependence and independence:

1. Through self-awareness

2. Open and honest communication
3. Set boundaries
4. Develop coping strategies
5. Work on building a secure attachment style
6. Build self-esteem and self-confidence

Practical strategies and actionable tips to help you work on these points and achieve that balance between dependence and independence are discussed in greater depth in other parts of this book.

Progress may be gradual, and setbacks can occur. It is important to maintain a compassionate and non-judgmental attitude toward each other as you both work on your attachment patterns. By actively addressing and supporting each other's growth, you can create a more secure and fulfilling relationship over time.

A Journey to Independence

The journey to independence in a relationship fraught with anxious attachment is a long, but rewarding one. And while you may feel that it is a hopeless pursuit at times, achieving independence in a relationship can be incredibly empowering and bring about a sense of self that is not reliant on external approval.

For anxious attachers, understanding your attachment pattern is key for personal growth and happiness. This does not have to be the end of your relationship. You can succeed in overcoming your anxious attachment by changing your behaviors and negative thoughts that dominate your relationship.

Self-Reflection and Awareness

For many anxious attachers, the journey to independence starts with self-reflection and awareness as you dedicate time to understanding the origins of your anxious attachment and the impact it has on your life and your relationships. Using the tools and techniques you have learned throughout this book, it is possible to differentiate between your past experiences and your current relationships.

Building a Strong Foundation

Anxious attachers cannot build a sense of independence without first building a strong foundation of self-worth and self-compassion. Focus on silencing your inner critic and practice self-care. We will be covering suggested methods for building a strong foundation in the following chapters.

Setting Healthy Boundaries

One of the more crucial steps in any journey to independence is to set healthy boundaries in your relationships. Learn to communicate your needs and expectations openly with your partner, and see how this newfound assertiveness helps you balance your desire for closeness with the need for personal space and autonomy in your relationships.

A Quest for Security

With fear of abandonment and rejection haunting your every step, it is easy to feel like you cannot engage in your romantic and other relationships. Being well aware of your anxious attachment style, and the toll it can take on your emotional independence is important as you dream of finding inner peace and security in your relationship.

Embracing Personal Growth

With each step on this journey, you will see your confidence grow as you once again pursue your interests and goals with a newfound passion. This is also a great time to pick up an old hobby that fell by the wayside or to discover a new one that you were not confident enough for before. These endeavors can help you discover your unique identity outside of your relationships.

Rewriting the Narrative

The journey to independence is about rewriting the narrative that governs your relationships. Challenge the stories you have told yourself - you know the ones where you told yourself you needed constant reassurance and validation to be loved.

Embrace Vulnerability

Independence does not mean closing yourself off from others, but rather about being vulnerable enough to express your fears and insecurities without shame. When you learn to do this correctly, you may find that your partner, friends, and family better understand you and can appropriately support you, ultimately fostering deeper connections.

Trust the Process

The path to independence is not a linear one. Learn to trust the process, accept that setbacks and moments of anxiety are all a part of this journey, and that you, too, should see these moments not as failures but as opportunities for growth.

The Power of Independence in Relationships

The harder you work, and the more dedicated you are to overcoming the challenges of your anxious attachment, the bigger the shift in all your relationships. Your independence can allow you to love and connect with others from a place of security rather than fear as you no longer rely on your partner to validate your worth. You can learn to value yourself independently.

Embracing the Journey

No journey is possible without its challenges. And while there may be setbacks and moments of doubt, perseverance is key.

The path to independence is not a destination but rather an ongoing process of growth and self-discovery filled with self-awareness and self-compassion.

Interdependence and Anxious Attachment

Interdependence is a state in which individuals rely on one another within the relationships while maintaining autonomy and independence. It is a balanced and healthy form of mutual reliance that sees both partners contributing to the relationship without sacrificing their individuality.

Anxious attachers often struggle with interdependence as their attachment fears and insecurities manifest in ways that hinder their ability to engage in healthy, balanced, and interdependent relationships.

There is some good news, though, as individuals with anxious attachment can learn to embrace healthier relationship dynamics. While anxious attachment and interdependence may initially appear incompatible, they can coexist harmoniously in a relationship with effort, communication, and self-work.

It is wholly important to address your attachment needs while also fostering a sense of autonomy and independence. When these elements come together, what you're left with is a healthy and fulfilling partnership.

Final Thoughts

For those with an anxious attachment style, the struggle between dependence and independence is a constant emotional battle. Often craving the safety and reassurance that come with dependence on their partners, this dependency can be a double-edged sword that leads to heightened anxiety and insecurity.

Finding the right balance between dependence and independence is essential for those with anxious attachment patterns. It's not about eradicating attachment needs, but rather transforming them into healthier, more secure forms of connection.

The key takeaways of this chapter are:

- Self-awareness is key to finding the balance that allows you to identify when you're leaning too heavily on dependence and when you might need to cultivate independence.

- Open and honest communication is vital to expressing your needs, fears, and insecurities. Also take the time to listen to what your partner has to say and what their boundaries are.

- Set healthy boundaries and respect those of your partner. These are truly the guardrails of healthy relationships. Knowing where you end and your partner begins is crucial for finding a healthy balance. Set boundaries that protect your emotional well-being while allowing room for some intimacy, too.

- Cultivate independence by actively pursuing your personal interests, goals, and hobbies outside of your relationships. Build a life that's fulfilling on its own to strengthen your sense of self.

The journey to balance dependence and independence is also the path towards a secure attachment. Learn to trust in yourself and your relationships to achieve greater emotional stability, resilience, and happiness.

Finding balance is a lifelong endeavor. There may be many setbacks and moments of struggle. And yes, there may also be times when you revert to your old patterns of thinking and behaviors. But, with patience, self-compassion, and dedication to growth, you will continue moving forward as your old thought patterns become less frequent and less intense until they eventually disappear. Don't let your attachment style rule your life or your relationship. Take control and implement the changes that see you becoming more independent, secure, and emotionally resilient.

Chapter Five: How to Change Your Behavior for Good with Cognitive Behavioral Therapy

॰॰॰

We're on to the juicy part of the book now as we look into the various therapies and treatment solutions that can help you tackle your anxious attachment head-on and change your behavior - for good!

While previous chapters focused on what anxious attachment is, and how it affects the various relationships in your life, the rest of our book will explore treatment options that work.

First up on the list is something you may have heard of or seen people put in practice but never been able to define - cognitive behavioral therapy (or CBT). This is by no means a new approach and was first introduced by American psychiatrist Aaron Beck as an alternative approach to treating and possibly curing anxiety and depression disorders.

With many of these issues previously only treated with extensive and costly therapies and medications, Beck's cognitive behavioral therapy was, at first, heavily criticized as many in the mental health care profession felt that CBT only treated the symptoms while ignoring the root cause or underlying issues. But, be that as it may, it has been adopted as a successful and popular therapy technique that has helped thousands of people - and you can be one of them.

Cognitive Behavioral Therapy: What is It?

CBT is, essentially, a cognitive toolkit that can help you reshape your behaviors and thinking, possibly transforming your life in the process. Based on the idea that the mind can be tricked into changing thought patterns and other learned behaviors, CBT relies on a number of strategies that will:

- Help you recognize the distortion in your thinking
- Reevaluate this distorted thinking
- Change your thinking patterns and behaviors (permanently)

The psychology behind CBT is that your feelings, thoughts, actions, and behaviors are all interconnected. Changing these feelings and behaviors is key to breaking free from the clutches of many psychological issues, and is why it is commonly recommended as an effective treatment option for anxious attachment.

Navigating Attachment Anxiety with CBT

Attachment plays a pivotal role in shaping our emotional well-being. And for those who grapple with anxious attachment, there is a constant undercurrent of anxiety and uncertainty that makes the quest for secure and fulfilling connections somewhat of a challenge.

Understanding the principles, benefits and techniques of CBT is vital to see that it is indeed a light in the darkness for many who suffer from anxious attachment. By examining and reshaping the cognitive patterns and modifying the behaviors that are so common with anxious attachment, you can break free from the constraints of your attachment and nurture healthier, more secure relationships with your partner and loved ones.

Cognitive behavioral therapy will empower you to see yourself and your relationships in a new light while fostering emotional resilience, self-awareness and understanding, and a greater sense of security in your relationship.

But, it extends beyond just restructuring and modifying behaviors as it encourages a transformation that encourages individuals to embrace mindfulness and self-compassion, ultimately helping them become more attuned to their emotions and allowing them to navigate their attachment-related anxieties with grace and understanding. Use CBT to learn to treat yourself with kindness while appreciating all that you have to offer.

In the pursuit of a secure attachment, CBT is a formidable ally, and as we explore all that this tool has to offer, we invite you to harness the potential of cognitive behavioral therapy as you embark on a journey toward a secure and fulfilling relationship.

The Benefits of Cognitive Behavioral Therapy

Cognitive behavioral therapy has been heralded as a beacon of hope for those with anxious attachment, as it teaches those who suffer from this attachment style to challenge their thoughts and emotions and ultimately change their behavior.

And with its focus on leading you to a brighter, more resilient and emotionally balanced future, CBT is fast becoming the therapy of choice for many individuals who need help dealing with anxiety and other psychological issues that ultimately affect their relationships with their partners, family, friends, and anyone else they come into contact with regularly.

But why is it so popular, and just what are the benefits of choosing CBT as a treatment option to heal from anxious attachment and develop secure attachments? Some of the biggest benefits include:

- Empowering self-awareness
- Effective problem solving
- Resilience and emotional regulation
- Better relationships
- Lasting change and a better quality of life

At some point or another, depression may arise, and this is where CBT comes in as it offers a reliable and highly recommended treatment plan for those with anxious attachment and a number of other psychological issues. As you shed the burdens of your anxiety and depression, you may just feel a sense of joy, purpose, and sense of fulfillment creeping in.

The Principles of Cognitive Behavioral Therapy

Now that we have a better idea of what CBT entails, let's look at the principles surrounding this therapy technique that could be the answer you have been looking for.

The core principles of CBT are:

#1: Cognition and Emotional Interaction

CBT focuses on the idea that our thoughts directly influence not only our emotions but our behaviors, too. How we interpret what we are going through, rather than the actual event, has the biggest impact on our emotions and behavior, and is what CBT focuses on changing.

Our emotions and behaviors influence our thoughts, and vice versa. By addressing and modifying our thoughts and behaviors, we can change our emotional responses to certain events, situations, and triggers.

#2: Identifying Negative Thought Patterns

Identifying and recognizing the negative thought patterns that stem from issues like anxious attachment and other psychological diagnoses is necessary to change the current thoughts and behaviors.

Anxious attachment leads to negative thoughts that, in turn, lead to emotional distress and problematic behaviors. These "negative thoughts", or distortions as professionals like to call them, include all-or-nothing thinking, catastrophizing, and personalization. The very first step in cognitive behavioral therapy is to recognize and challenge these distorted thought patterns.

#3: The ABC Model

The ABC Model is made up of the following aspects:

A: Activating Event
B: Beliefs
C: Consequences

This model is based on the principle that your beliefs and the associated consequences are a direct result of the activating event. In anxious attachment, these beliefs and consequences are caused by attachment issues formed during childhood or as a result of trauma you endured in these all-important formative years.

#4: Changing Thought Patterns

Once you have identified the negative thought patterns that arise from your anxious attachment, CBT can help you change how you think and react to certain events or triggers.

#5: Changing Behaviors

Cognitive behavioral therapy addresses the problematic behaviors and helps you develop healthier coping strategies and behavioral responses to your triggers.

#6: Homework and Skill-Building Assignments

CBT requires a bit of homework as you self-evaluate your thinking and behaviors and actively do exercises that can help you change the way you think. CBT provides practical tools to help you manage your anxious attachment.

Putting Cognitive Behavioral Therapy Into Practice

Cognitive behavioral therapy has been used to treat any number of psychological issues and will help you to overcome your anxious attachment and its resulting thoughts and behaviors. Putting this into practice is generally done over three steps:

- Assessment
- Intervention
- Evaluation

Let's discuss the following points in more depth below to help you overcome your challenges and say goodbye to anxious attachment for good:

1. Identifying negative thought patterns
2. Challenging cognitive distortions
3. Developing coping strategies
4. Changing behavior
5. Developing secure attachment
6. Maintaining your progress

Identifying Negative Thought Patterns

The first step in changing your behavior is to identify any negative thought patterns. These thought patterns can creep in at any time, and are bound to fuel your anxious attachment even further.

When your anxiety sets in or you have experienced something that triggers your emotional attachment, try to take note in that very moment, of how you are feeling, and any thoughts you may be having. There are plenty of great smartphone apps available that can help you conveniently and quickly track thoughts and emotions over time. A pen and paper can work just as well. Do you see a pattern emerging? Is there a specific trigger that stands out above the rest? This is what you should be working on to manage.

Challenging Cognitive Distortions

To put this in simpler terms, the second step in managing your anxious attachment is to challenge your thinking and feelings of anxiety. Assuming the worst, believing that you know what the other person is thinking, and blaming yourself for things that are not your fault are all common cognitive distortions that those with anxious attachment are prone to, so it is time to push those aside and let yourself heal.

If your common behavior is to assume the worst, stop overthinking things and take what people say at face value. A good example is when a friend does not respond to your text. This can quickly lead to you assuming that they do not want to speak to you, that they are angry with you, or that you have done something wrong and do not deserve a reply.

Challenge your own thinking by coming up with other reasons for their silence. Perhaps they are just busy and have not seen your text yet. So often we focus on the what-ifs that we forget that things are not always as bad as we think they are.

Developing Coping Strategies

CBT can help you develop coping strategies that see you thinking and behaving differently. From breathing exercises and mindfulness to reducing anxiety levels, there is a lot to be said for CBT techniques.

One of the most important strategies that CBT can teach you is to be assertive in your thinking and actions. Assertively expressing your thoughts and feelings is far better than turning into an emotional train wreck or exploding into a burst of anger.

Here are a few tips on how to be more assertive:

- **Identify your feelings and needs**: Using the ABC model, identify what the Action is, how it made you feel or Believe, and what the Consequences are of not asserting yourself in this situation. Take control of the situation and watch the rest come together.

- **Use "I" statements**: always start your statement with "I." A good example of this is to choose your words carefully when expressing your frustrations. Say this, "I feel frustrated when..." rather than "You make me so angry or frustrated when..."

- **Practice active refusal:** Learn how and when to say "no" without feeling guilty. It is okay to say no to something that doesn't align with your needs or priorities.

- **Ask for feedback:** Ask your friends, family members, or even your colleagues for feedback on your assertiveness skills and where they think you can improve.

- **Listen**: Practice active listening rather than just focusing on the negative. Let your partner/friend/family member express themselves and attentively listen to what they have to say without getting defensive and thinking that they are blaming you.

- **Stay calm**: Getting angry won't help your situation. Remain calm and keep your emotions in check as you explain why you are upset. Maintain eye contact too, as this can show the other person that you are confident in what you are saying.

- **Set realistic expectations**: Not everyone will be as open or receptive to your new-found assertiveness as you hoped. Keep this in mind and do not make any extreme demands or try to control their actions and behaviors.

- **Pick your battles:** Depending on what your triggers are, there are going to be times when you need to stop, take a step back, and evaluate whether the issue you are dealing with is worth the battle. If it is something that you can solve on your own using one of the many CBT techniques we have outlined, then leave it out of the argument.

These tips might seem like things that you are already doing, but they can make a world of difference. Practice them often and see how your assertiveness soars.

Changing Your Behavior

Healing and developing a secure attachment are only possible if you change the behaviors you are currently displaying. Constantly seeking reassurance, monitoring your partner's every move, and displaying jealousy are all common traits of someone with anxious attachment and these need to be changed in order to develop more secure attachments with your partner, friends, and family members.

Take a second to think something through before charging at your partner like a bull in a china shop and use "I" statements to identify just what it is that you want or need. Change is possible if you really want to get over your anxious attachment and build a better relationship with your partner and loved ones.

Maintaining Your Progress

Healing is an ongoing process and definitely does not come overnight. You need to keep working on identifying the thought patterns and behaviors that you typically display when your anxiety is triggered, and understanding why you are behaving in a certain way.

Keep adding to your journal, and do not make the mistake of thinking you are suddenly healed when you close this book. Continue to monitor your thoughts, feelings, and behaviors, and address any issues as they come up.

Practice your affirmations, reach out to your therapist, have a heart-to-heart with your partner or loved ones, and regularly check in with yourself to assess how you are doing.

CBT Exercises: What to do

Here are some of the most common CBT exercises you can try to help you overcome your anxious attachment:

1. A Thought Record

This first exercise involves keeping a journal to track and analyze your thoughts, emotions, behaviors, and triggers. A journal can help you identify irrational or negative thought patterns, help you understand what your main triggers are, and help you replace negative thoughts with more rational and positive ones.

- **The Event**: Identify or write down the situation: Describe what triggered your anxiety or caused negative thoughts.
- **Your Emotions**: Write a brief description of what you are feeling and rate them on a scale of 1 to 10.
- **Your Thoughts**: List all your thoughts, both positive and negative, about the situation.
- **Reasoning**: This is a tricky one as you need to look at facts and analyze if your thoughts are truly warranted in that situation.
- **Alternative Thoughts**: Jot down a few more rational or balanced thoughts based on your reasoning above.

- **Re-Rate Your Emotions**: Re-evaluate your emotions after considering the alternative thoughts you have identified.

2. Behavioral Exercises

These exercises involve testing your beliefs and assumptions through real-life actions.

Here are a few examples of behavioral exercises you can try to help change your negative thought patterns and challenge your anxious attachment:

1. **Reassurance reduction.** Commit to reducing how often you seek reassurance from your partner. For example, if you are texting your partner a few times a day to check if everything is okay, decrease this to once a day or less.
2. **Scheduled check-ins.** Rather than seeking reassurance impulsively, schedule a time for you and your partner to have a check-in. This gives you a set time to discuss your concerns and feelings without overwhelming your partner with constant requests.
3. **Mindful delay.** Before reaching out to your partner to seek reassurance, take a moment to breathe deeply and assess whether your concerns are genuine or if they are driven by anxiety.

4. **Self-soothing strategies.** Deep breathing exercises, meditation, or doing something you love on your own can help you learn to self-soothe and tackle your anxiety head-on. Self-soothing is very much an individual practice, and while one thing might work for one person, another might not. Think about what you like to do to self-soothe - whether it's going for a walk to clear your head, practicing deep-breathing exercises, or doing some meditation.

Over time, behavioral exercises can help you develop more secure and balanced behaviors in your relationship. Practice these exercises often.

3. Graded Exposure

Also known as systematic desensitization or exposure therapy, this is a great exercise for those with anxious attachment and other anxiety disorders and involves the sufferer gradually exposing themselves to the feared situation. Doing so can help you desensitize your fear response over time.

One of the more common fears that those with anxious attachment face is the fear of abandonment or being alone. You can try graded exposure by scheduling time away from your partner. The trick is to make it fun and to do something that will distract you from your negative thought patterns. Buy a movie ticket, go to a show, plan a walk, or go shopping to keep yourself busy and occupy your mind.

4. Activity Scheduling

Create a daily or weekly schedule of activities that bring you happiness. Be sure to choose things that you enjoy, that help you combat depression, and increase your motivation to change your negative thought patterns.

A walk, or jog, in nature can help increase endorphins and boost your mood significantly. Plan a walk with a friend, or, if you have one, take your dog on a walk in a park for some fresh air and some much-needed Vitamin D. Having a scheduled activity, much like a date, is a helpful and necessary distraction to keep you from fixating on the negative thoughts that often seem to rule your anxious attachment.

5. Meditation

Whether you believe in it or not, meditation is a great mindfulness technique that helps you become aware of your thoughts and feelings. There are a number of mobile apps that offer guided meditation, so use these to help you practice mindful meditation to overcome your anxious attachment and improve your overall well-being.

In the next chapter, we will give you a more in-depth look at guided meditation. For now, though, we encourage you to take up meditation to help you clear your mind of all negative thoughts and practice grounding techniques. Download a meditation app, get comfortable, close your eyes, and free your mind of all your troublesome thoughts and negative thought patterns.

6. Cognitive Restructuring

This forms the basis of CBT and helps you identify and challenge those negative thoughts that plague you. Practice cognitive restructuring by asking yourself questions like, "Is there evidence to support this thought or feeling?" when you feel that all-too-familiar anxiety creeping in.

Cognitive restructuring may take some practice to learn, but the benefits of this technique speak for themselves. Here's how to put cognitive restructuring into practice:

1. **Identify the thought.** For this example, we will use the anxiety that many anxious attachers feel when their partner doesn't respond to their text. In step one, identify the negative thought.
2. **Question the thought.** Asking yourself a few questions will help challenge the validity of the thought. These questions can include:

a. Is there any validity to my thoughts that my partner is going to leave me simply because they are not responding to my texts?
   b. Have there been times when my partner has had a valid reason for not responding immediately?
   c. Have their previous reasons ever had anything to do with the relationship?
3. **Create alternative thoughts.** This is the time that you can create more rational, balanced thoughts. These include:
   a. My partner has a busy schedule and there could be many reasons for the delay in response.
   b. Our relationship is built on trust and communication. A delayed text does not mean that they are abandoning me or losing interest in me.
4. **Implement some behavioral changes.** Based on your new, more balanced thoughts, remain patient and understanding as you engage in self-soothing techniques such as deep breathing or mindfulness to manage your anxiety.

Cognitive restructuring can help you challenge and change irrational beliefs, reduce your anxiety, and improve your overall emotional well-being and the quality of your relationship.

7. Muscle Relaxation

Tensing and relaxing different muscle groups can help you reduce any physical tension you may have and promote relaxation. This helps with anxiety and stress. A video on guided meditation can help you with this technique, or you can follow the steps below.

1. **Find a quiet space where you won't be disturbed.** Close the door, shut out all outside noise, and ensure you won't be disturbed by a ringing phone.
2. **Find a comfortable position.** Whether you prefer to sit or lie down, finding a comfortable position will help you relax.
3. **Start with deep breathing.** Inhale deeply through your nose for a count of four, hold your breath for a count of four, and exhale slowly through your mouth for a count of six. Focus on the rhythm of your breathing.
4. **Implement progressive muscle relaxation.** Start at your feet, working your way up through your body. Tense each muscle group for a few seconds before you release them, paying close attention to the physical sensations this provides. For examples:
    a. Start with the toes, curling them tight for a few seconds before releasing.
    b. Move up to your calf muscles. Tighten and release them.

c. Continue with your thighs, buttocks, abdomen, chest, back, arms, and neck, tensing and releasing each muscle group for a few seconds.

Muscle relaxation techniques can help you address both the physical and emotional aspects of your anxiety. Over time, and with practice, these muscle relaxation techniques will become an invaluable tool for managing your attachment-related anxieties and will promote emotional well-being.

8. Thought-Stopping

This is an interesting technique as it involves using a physical or mental cue to help you stop those negative thoughts in their tracks. You can say, "STOP!" or visualize a red stop sign.

For this technique, we will once again use the example of your partner's delayed response to your text to explain how to practice thought-stopping. Here's what to do:

1. **Recognize that you're experiencing anxiety.** Self-awareness is key in this scenario as it helps you identify and realize that you are having intrusive thoughts.
2. **Choose a physical cue.** Snap your fingers, clap your hands, put your hand out in front of you - no matter which physical cue you choose, a physical gesture can become a signal you use to stop the anxious thoughts.

3. **Interrupt the thought.** As soon as you notice the anxious thought, use your chosen physical cue to interrupt it.
4. **Replace the thought.** You can change the way you think by replacing negative thoughts with rational ones. For example:
    a. Replace "they must be angry with me" with "there could be various reasons for the delay, and it is not necessarily about me."
    b. Replace "they're probably losing interest in me" with "our relationship has been strong, and occasional delays are normal."
5. **Use positive affirmations.** Once you have replaced the thought, repeat a positive affirmation that will reinforce your new perspective. A good example of this is, "I trust in our connection, and my partner's actions do not define my worth."

By practicing thought-stopping, you can gain better control over your intrusive thoughts and prevent them from escalating.

9. Self-monitoring

Self-monitoring involves keeping a diary or journal to help track your thoughts, emotions, and behaviors over a period of time. Use these entries to help you identify patterns or triggers for your anxious attachment.

Here are a few helpful steps you can follow to put this useful technique into practice:

1. **Identify the behavior or trigger you want to monitor.** Write it down and acknowledge what it is you want to change.
2. **Set clear goals for yourself.** For example, if you want to focus on increasing your emotional resilience to one of your triggers, define the outcome to stay focused.
3. **Choose a tracking method.** A physical journal, mobile application, spreadsheet, or voice recording app to verbally record your observations or thoughts are all great options. Choose one that you are most comfortable with.
4. **Define the parameters.** Including information like the date, time, emotional state, and trigger is helpful to keep track of what is going on and how you plan to change the negative behaviors or thoughts. Keep your goal in mind, and track as much as you possibly can.
5. **Establish a routine.** Set aside some time for self-monitoring. Consistency is key in identifying the triggers and behaviors that you want to analyze. Whether you do it daily, weekly, or on an ad-hoc basis, it is necessary to keep up with your routine.

6. **Record your data.** Actively record your thoughts, feelings, and emotions. Be honest and objective, focusing rather on the event than on self-criticism or judgment.
7. **Review your entries.** It is helpful to go back and read through your entries from time to time. Identify triggers or patterns that jump out at you and come up with strategies or techniques to tackle these head-on or find solutions.
8. **Set goals for improvement.** Once you have identified a pattern or triggers, set clear, achievable goals for improvement or change. These goals should give you guidance on what you need to work on.
9. **Be patient.** Self-monitoring takes time, and you cannot expect to see changes overnight. Be patient with yourself and acknowledge that change and improvement are a work in progress.

Self-monitoring can be a valuable tool for self-improvement and self-awareness while tackling your anxious attachment. It can help you gain helpful insights into your thought patterns, emotions, and behaviors, ultimately empowering you to make positive changes and achieve personal growth.

For emotions that can't be journaled, use self-awareness to make mental notes that you can refer back to when the same emotion is stirred up.

10. Social skills training

Social skills might prove difficult for individuals with anxious attachment. Social skills training involves learning and practicing certain specific social skills like active listening, assertiveness, and the value of clear and effective communication.

There are a number of social skills that can help you manage your anxious attachment and kick those intrusive thoughts and anxieties to the curb. Here are a few that we suggest you try today:

1. **Active listening.** Practice maintaining eye contact, nodding, and using verbal cues like "I see," or "tell me more" to show that you are both interested and understand what your partner or someone else is telling you.
2. **Empathy.** Work on developing empathy by putting yourself in your partner's shoes during role-playing exercises. This will help you learn to consider their perspective, feelings, and needs in your interactions with your partner and those you love.
3. **Assertive communication.** Practice expressing your thoughts, feelings, and needs clearly and in a respectful

manner. Learn to use "I" statements when doing so, and make sure to avoid blame and accusations.

4. **Positive self-talk.** Work on changing negative self-talk patterns that contribute to your anxious attachment. Affirmations and cognitive restructuring can help you replace self-critical thoughts with self-compassionate and self-affirming statements.

5. **Self-monitoring.** Track your progress by monitoring your communication and interactions. Note instances where you have successfully implemented the skills you have learned, and identify those areas where you feel you can continue to improve or need to work a little harder.

Social skills training can help those with anxious attachment develop healthier communication patterns, build more secure relationships, and reduce the anxiety and clinginess that comes with anxious attachment. Over time, these improved social skills can lead to more emotionally secure connections with others.

Self-Help Cognitive Behavioral Therapy

CBT can be used as a self-help tool to help you manage and possibly overcome your anxious attachment. And while some believe that it is only possible to approach CBT with the guidance of a trained therapist, it is very important to remember that therapists themselves cannot rewire the neural connections made during your early years that have resulted in anxious attachment. Much like this book, they can, however, give you the tools you need to do the work yourself, which, at an older age, can take a little more time and perseverance.

Self-help cognitive behavioral therapy is available in the following forms:

Books and Resources

There are a great number of self-help books (this one included), online resources, and mobile apps that provide valuable information and exercises based on the core principles of cognitive behavioral therapy. These can help you gain a basic understanding of the CBT techniques, and how to apply them to your specific concerns.

Self-Guided Practice

Self-help CBT materials provide tips and tricks to work on specific issues like managing stress, anxiety, or mild depression. These materials can help you learn more about cognitive restructuring, behavior modification, and other techniques that can help you address your specific challenges.

Daily Practices

Self-help CBT often involves daily or regular practices like journaling, self-monitoring, or relaxation exercises that you can integrate into your routine.

Self-help CBT is a valuable starting point for your personal growth, and can help you manage everyday stress.

Final Thoughts

These CBT exercises are an excellent tool for those struggling with anxious attachment, and will equip you with the practical skills to address its root causes. By identifying and challenging your negative thought patterns and behaviors, you will gain insight into your attachment style and learn to manage your anxieties independently.

Cognitive behavioral therapy provides a structured framework for recognizing and replacing irrational beliefs with more rational and constructive ones, helping you build your self-confidence and emotional resilience. These resources and techniques will enable you to take charge of your personal growth and emotional well-being, empowering you to develop healthier, more secure attachment patterns and improve the quality of your relationships.

Chapter Six: Schema Therapy - An Effective Tool to Combat Anxious Attachment

※

In the pursuit of love and connection, our desire for intimacy, security, and validation is a driving force that shapes the course of our lives and also our relationships. For some, and especially for those with an anxious attachment style, this pursuit can become a relentless tug-of-war between the longing for closeness and the fear of abandonment. This is often the reality for those with anxious attachment.

This chapter introduces you to another therapeutic approach that holds the promise of breaking the chains of anxious attachment as it guides you toward more secure, fulfilling and resilient connections.

This is schema therapy.

First introduced to the world by Dr. Jeffrey Young, schema therapy is a combination of cognitive behavioral therapy, psychodynamic therapy, and attachment theory. It recognizes that our attachment patterns, often deeply ingrained in our early years, shape our emotions and influence the way we relate to others.

Schema therapy has its roots firmly planted in understanding maladaptive schemas. What is a schema, you ask? A schema is a deep-seated, negative belief about yourself and the world.

Let's look at the principles of this therapeutic approach and how it can help you overcome your anxious attachment.

Schema Therapy: What You Should Know

Dr. Young developed his schema therapy to create a more comprehensive and flexible therapeutic approach to addressing the complex and persistent issues that those with emotional difficulties, like anxious attachment, face.

He based his approach on the following key principles or components:

Identification of Early Maladaptive Schemas

The primary focus of schema therapy is to identify and address early maladaptive schemas (EMS). These are deeply ingrained core beliefs about yourself, others, and the world that are developed during childhood. EMS are formed when core or emotional needs are not adequately or properly met and have a profound impact on your thoughts, feelings, behaviors, and relationships.

The most common EMS identified by schema therapy are:

Abandonment or Instability
This schema revolves around the belief that the most important people in your life will abandon you, leading to fear of rejection, abandonment, and instability in your relationships.

Emotional deprivation
People with this schema often feel that their emotional needs will never be met by others, and this can lead to chronic feelings of loneliness and longing for emotional connection. It is this schema, too, that might be responsible for the desire for intimacy.

Defectiveness or Shame
This schema involves the belief that you are fundamentally flawed or defective because of your anxious attachment. This often leads to feelings of shame, self-criticism, and a feeling of inadequacy or that you are unworthy of love.

Social Isolation

Feeling that you don't belong, or that you will never fit in is just one of the challenges of anxious attachment. Schema therapy tackles these feelings head-on.

Emotional Inhibition

Schema therapy describes emotional inhibition as suppressing your own emotions in a bid to avoid conflict or disapproval from others, which leads to difficulties in expressing your emotions and forming secure attachments with those in your life.

Negativity or Pessimism

Anxious attachment is defined by negative thought patterns and will lead you to hyperfocus on the negative aspects of your life or relationships.

Identifying and addressing early maladaptive schemas is a central focus of schema therapy. By exploring these schemas, challenging negative beliefs, and developing healthier coping strategies to overcome your anxious attachment, you, too, can experience profound emotional healing and growth.

The Core Principles of Schema Therapy

Schema therapy is grounded in the following principles:

1. Identifying early maladaptive schemas. We have identified the more common schemas of those with anxious attachment above.

2. Understanding schema origins. Exploring the origin of the schemas associated with anxious attachment can be a key step in changing them.

3. Challenging negative beliefs. Schema therapy will teach you various techniques to challenge and modify your negative beliefs and thought patterns. Cognitive restructuring is a core principle of cognitive behavioral therapy, but it is also a technique used in schema therapy.

4. Emotional processing. This therapy process includes emotional processing, allowing you to express and process the deep emotions associated with your anxious attachment.

5. Behavioral change. Schema therapy emphasizes behavioral change as it teaches you new ways of behaving in your relationship. This includes setting healthy boundaries, communicating assertively, and reducing your reliance on others for constant reassurance.

6. Reparenting. A unique aspect of schema therapy is the concept of reparenting. This involves learning to provide yourself with the care and nurturing that you may not have received in childhood. Self-soothing and self-compassion are essential for those with anxious attachment.

7. Experiential Techniques. Imagery exercises can help you confront and work through those unresolved emotional issues related to your anxious attachment.

8. Homework and Skill Building. Like other forms of therapy, schema therapy involves homework assignments and skill-building exercises to practice new ways of thinking and behaving in everyday life.

9. Integration. The ultimate goal of schema therapy is to help you integrate healthier beliefs and behaviors into your daily life, fostering more secure attachment patterns and improving overall well-being.

Schema therapy is typically conducted over a period of time, sometimes months or even years, as it involves deep and transformative work.

Schema Therapy as a Self-Help Tool

While some would say that schema therapy should only be attempted with the help of a professional therapist, it is possible to use this therapy as a self-help tool.

There are a number of self-help materials and resources available that can provide valuable insights and exercises for those looking to address their anxious attachment and early maladaptive schemas on their own.

Here are a few that are worth your time and effort:

1. **Online Resources**

There are two fantastic online resources that you can visit for information, articles, and resources, including self-help materials and worksheets. They are:

- SchemaTherapy.com
  This is the official website for schema therapy, and is the go-to resource for those who want to learn more about Schema and its benefits. You can access the website at www.schematherapy.com.
- The Schema Therapy Society
  The society's website provides additional resources and information about schema therapy. Access the society's website by visiting www.schematherapysociety.org.

2. Mindfulness and Self-Compassion Practices

These practices can help you become more aware of your emotions and develop self-soothing skills.

3. Journaling

Keeping a journal can help you track your thoughts, emotions, and behaviors related to anxious attachment. Use your journal to identify patterns and work through your emotions.

4. Online Forums and Support Groups

Online communities are a great resource to provide support and the opportunity to share experiences with others who are also working on their attachment issues.

Now that you have a basic idea of what schema therapy is, let's take a quick look at some of the benefits of this therapy technique as a tool to manage and possibly overcome your anxious attachment.

The Benefits of Schema Therapy

Schema therapy is a highly effective approach for those seeking to address the emotional issues that stem from anxious attachment. Here are a few of the key benefits:

- In-depth understanding of your emotional needs

- Transformation of maladaptive patterns
- Emotional healing
- Development of coping strategies
- Improved relationships
- Long-lasting behavioral change
- Personal growth

Overall, schema therapy offers a comprehensive approach to addressing complex emotional and psychological issues as it focuses on understanding and transforming the early maladaptive schemas, making it particularly effective in promoting lasting change and emotional well-being while tackling the issues associated with anxious attachment.

Schema Therapy Exercises You Should Try

A self-help book is only effective when it provides tips and tricks that you can try at home. And this book is no different.

We have looked at what schema therapy is, the core principles of this therapy technique, and its benefits. Now it is time to look at just how you can use schema therapy to help you manage, modify, and overcome the negative thought patterns, emotions and behaviors associated with your anxious attachment.

Exercise 1: Schema Mode Journaling

The first exercise on our list requires you to keep a journal where you document your thoughts, feelings, and behaviors in different situations. Just as you would monitor or track patterns of behavior or triggers during cognitive behavioral therapy, so too would you pay attention to the moments that stand out as strong emotional reactions or maladaptive patterns.

Identify which schema mode is activated during these moments. For example, are you in the defensive or vulnerable mode where you feel unworthy of love and fear rejection? Reflect on the thoughts and beliefs associated with the mode you are in, and consider how these could be influencing your reactions.

Self-awareness is key in this exercise as you identify, understand, and acknowledge your thoughts, feelings, and behaviors.

Exercise 2: Chair Work
This is a great technique that can help you role-play a situation on your own, expressing the thoughts and emotions associated with your reaction or feelings.

Place two chairs facing each other, and imagine sitting in each chair to represent yourself and your partner or loved one. Engage in a dialogue between the two chairs, imagining that you are having an open and honest conversation with your partner about how you are feeling and why you could be feeling the way you are.

Chair work is effective in helping you identify your behaviors and acknowledge the cause of your negative thought patterns.

Exercise 3: Behavioral Experiments
This exercise involves experimenting with changing your behavior in a specific situation to challenge a negative thought pattern or maladaptive schema. A good example of this is practicing assertive communication in a situation where you would normally try to avoid conflict. Take some time to think about your emotions and reactions during and after the experiment.

Here's an example: Your partner has come home late with no indication as to where they were or who they were with. This is a trigger for you as you fear they will lose interest in you or abandon you for someone better. How would you typically respond to this?

For many anxious attachers, this could send them spiraling into self-doubt, an argument with their partner, or simply retreating within themselves and bottling up their emotions. This is not the time to shy away from your emotions, but rather to embrace them as you tackle your trigger head-on.

Sit your partner down and calmly and clearly express that you are upset. Rather than blaming them or accusing them, use "I" statements to let your partner know that you are feeling anxious about what has occurred. Explain how you are feeling, but try not to get upset. Tell them how you feel, and explain why their behavior has upset you, encouraging them to be open and honest with you.

Exercise 4: Imagery Techniques

Close your eyes and imagine a scenario that you would typically face due to your anxious attachment. For example, if you are struggling with your fear of abandonment, imagine a scenario where you feel abandoned. Pay attention to the emotions that you experience during this exercise, and then work on changing the imagery to create a more positive outcome or sense of self-soothing.

Exercise 5: Thought Records

A thought record is useful in tracking your negative thought patterns and behaviors as they happen. Include as many details as you can about the situation, emotions and schema that is activated.

Challenge these negative thoughts by looking for evidence that supports more balanced, rational, fact-based beliefs, and write these down.

Exercise 6: Self-Nurturing Exercises
Self-soothing and self-nurturing are necessary to address your needs and desires that stem from your anxious attachment. Great examples of these techniques include meditation, deep breathing, and engaging in hobbies that you may enjoy.

Think about what it is that calms you, and employ that tactic to help calm you down and self-soothe. For some, it may be taking deep breaths while running your fingers through your hair, while for others it might be taking a walk in the woods. There is no wrong or right way to self-soothe, so do what works for you.

Schema exercises are most effective when used consistently, so consider making these a part of your routine as you navigate your way through the complexities of your anxious attachment and find ways to adapt and modify your thinking and behavior.

Final Thoughts

As chapter five draws to a close we would like to acknowledge the important transformation that can take place when you confront the roots of your anxious attachment and its relevant anxieties and triggers.

In this chapter we've learned that anxious attachment is born of early maladaptive schemas, and that these do not need to be the life sentence you think they are. Instead, we have given you the tool to effectively modify your emotions, thinking, and behaviors - schema therapy.

Schema therapy focuses on the power of insight, understanding, and emotional healing. Once you have embraced the concepts of schema therapy, try out the exercises and see for yourself what a difference these techniques can make in changing your behaviors and moving toward making more secure attachments.

Remember that healing and transformation are within your reach. Your anxious attachment need not define your relationships in your life. You possess the capacity for change, resilience, and the deep, fulfilling connections you seek. Let schema therapy be one of the tools in your arsenal to help you unshackle your heart and create a brighter, more secure future.

Chapter Seven: The Power of Affirmations and Visualization

☙❧

Affirmations. What are they? And how can they help you change your thinking and overcome your anxious attachment? In this chapter, we'll explore the wonderful world of affirmations by defining what they are, looking at their benefits, and also seeing what science has to say about the power of affirmations. So without further ado, let's jump right in.

Affirmations: What Are They Really?

Simply put, affirmations are little phrases that you say to yourself to change your current thoughts or to hype yourself up. These positive phrases can be repeated as often as you need to hear them, can form a part of your morning or daily routine, and are known to help boost your confidence and leave you feeling powerful and ready to face just about any challenge.

It sounds easy enough, but can they really help you overcome your anxious attachment? Science says yes, and the idea of affirmations was explored by social psychologist Claude Steele in 1988 as a part of his self-affirmation theory.

Without getting into the nitty gritty, Steele's theory was based on the principle that we all have aspects of ourselves that we value. When one of these values is threatened or we take a knock to our self-confidence, we use another value to support it and build our value or self-integrity up again. Steele goes on to suggest that even two to three minutes of self-reflection and repeating a few positive self-affirmations can make a massive difference to your mental health.

The Benefits of Self-Affirmations

There is no point in doing something that doesn't benefit you or helps you overcome your anxious attachment, right? So now that we know what an affirmation is, let's look at the benefits of these powerful phrases and how they can be used to treat anxious attachment.

#1: Affirmations build self-esteem

Anxious attachment sufferers base much of their self-worth and value on external validation and approval or reassurance of others. Affirmations like, "I am worthy of love," "I love and accept myself as I am," and, "I am not my anxious attachment" encourage a more positive self-image by reinforcing that all-important self-love and self-worth. These simple yet powerful phrases can boost your confidence and reduce the need for validation or reassurance from others, giving you a better grasp of your own value and worth.

#2: Affirmations reduce self-doubt

Having an anxious attachment style leads to a lot of self-doubt and insecurity as you fear abandonment by your partner, friends, or even family members. Affirmations can help you counter these negative thought patterns by replacing them with positive and reassuring statements like, "I trust myself to handle challenges in my relationship," "My partner will not abandon me," "I am loved by my partner/friends/family members," "I am enough." The trick is to challenge those thoughts that lead to insecurity, and affirmations are a great way of doing so.

#3: Affirmations increase independence

Affirmations can help encourage self-reliance and independence - two things that are in rather short supply for someone with anxious attachment. Repeating statements like, "I am capable of taking care of myself," "I am self-sufficient and independent," and "I can do anything I put my mind to" can quickly remind you of your capabilities, leaving those feelings of anxiety in the dust where they belong.

#4: Affirmations help you cope with uncertainty

Anxious attachment sufferers struggle with a fair amount of uncertainty as they fear what lies ahead. Affirmations help manage this common anxiety by promoting a more balanced perspective. "I trust that I can handle whatever comes my way," and "I am able to cope with any changes in a positive way" are just two affirmations that may reduce the uncertainty of what lies ahead and also the fear of abandonment that you may often feel.

#5: Affirmations bring about mindfulness and presence

Much of the anxiety that you feel as a result of your anxious attachment arises when worrying about the past or the future. Affirmations are a mindful practice that forces you to focus on the here and now, bringing about a sense of calm and reducing those anxious thoughts. A simple phrase like, "I choose to focus on today without worrying about yesterday or tomorrow" is a great example of a positive affirmation that can help you change your mindset and bring about peace.

#6: Affirmations create positive relationship patterns

This may seem like a rather ridiculous statement. But, when you put it into perspective, it can make a lot of sense when you understand that affirmations help guide you toward a healthier relationship pattern as you learn to express yourself better. Learning and repeating affirmations like, "I communicate my needs and boundaries clearly" can reduce any misunderstandings and conflicts that so often arise in relationships.

#7: Affirmations help you attract healthy partners
Affirming your self-worth and learning to love yourself are the best ways to help you attract a healthy partner who can be supportive and respectful of your emotional needs and wants. Affirmations like, "I am worthy of love," "I am not difficult to love," and "I am a good partner" can help you value your self-worth, in turn helping you choose a partner that can alleviate your anxiety rather than exacerbate it.

These are all great benefits and only reinforce the idea that affirmations are the way to go to help you heal and overcome your anxious attachment. While it takes some time, and most definitely won't happen overnight, it is possible to learn some self-love and truly value yourself. The trick is to repeat your affirmations as often as possible and to genuinely believe what you are saying.

There is empirical evidence that shows that positive self-affirmation practices are beneficial to those with anxious attachment. While there is no rule as to how often you should be repeating these positive phrases, renowned psychotherapist Ronald Alexander from the Open Mind Training Institute in California recommends that affirmations be repeated at least three to five times a day for a full month before you start seeing the benefits.

He also recommends that you write them in a journal and practice them in the mirror to truly benefit from the power of self-affirmations.

Affirmations and Therapy: A Potent Combination

Affirmations are pretty powerful on their own, but are even more so when practiced in conjunction with another therapy as they form the basis of the cognitive restructuring that is needed to overcome anxious attachment and form secure attachments.

Combining affirmations with CBT is an even more powerful approach to addressing the various challenges of anxious attachment. With each having its own strengths, combining them creates a symbiotic relationship between the two that can have some powerful results.

Here are a few ways in which affirmations and CBT complement each other:

- **Positive self-image**: Affirmations focus on promoting a positive self-image and self-worth. When integrated into CBT, they can help you challenge your negative thought patterns and beliefs, replacing them with more positive perceptions that reinforce the cognitive restructuring aspect of cognitive behavioral therapy.

- **Increased self-awareness**: As you would have learned in chapter four, cognitive behavioral therapy helps identify and understand those negative thoughts that you may have as a result of your anxious attachment. Affirmations can further help this process as you learn to recognize when your thoughts are unhelpful or are self-sabotaging.

- **Motivation and goal-setting**: Affirmations are often used to set and reinforce goals that you want to achieve. These are more personal goals that focus on improving your self-worth, often motivating you to change how you feel and see things. Combining these affirmations with CBT can boost your motivation and commitment to the therapy process and remind you of the positive changes you want to make.

- **Stress reduction**: Affirmations help reduce stress levels and reduce anxiety by promoting self-soothing, self-love, and relaxation. This complements the techniques of CBT for managing anxiety. Breathing exercises, exposure therapy, and affirmations can all help you reduce your stress and manage your anxiety better.

- **Better coping strategies**: CBT does a great job of equipping individuals with practical coping strategies to deal with the challenges of anxious attachment and the negative emotions attached to it. Affirmations further reinforce these strategies and help you stay calm and resilient when faced with any setbacks or triggers.

- **Improved "self-talk"**: Affirmations encourage positive self-talk and self-encouragement. When combined with CBT, the positive messages of affirmations can counteract the negative self-talk and thinking, helping to change the thought patterns of an anxious attachment sufferer more effectively.

- **Resilience**: Affirmations and CBT both have the power to help you learn more long-term resilience in how you think, perceive certain things, and behave when faced with challenges. CBT equips you with the tools to address any specific issues, while affirmations help you achieve a more positive mental outlook and self-concept.

- **Personalization**: Affirmations can be changed to suit just about any challenge or issue that you may be facing as a result of your anxious attachment. CBT, too, can be personalized to suit your individual needs and challenges.

This allows you to directly target the issues you are working on in your CBT sessions.

And as with any treatment method, it is always important to note that what works for you might not necessarily work for someone else.

Combining affirmations and CBT is effective, but results can ultimately vary based on your unique needs and preferences. Therapists can be a useful resource for advice on how to use CBT and affirmations as tools to help you overcome anxious attachment, but always remember that consistent application of these tools outside the therapist's office and in your daily life is what leads to real progress over time.

Affirmations You Can Try

Let's now look at some of the best affirmations that you can use to help you overcome the challenges of your anxious attachment. To make it easier to know which to use when, we'll group them according to the different challenges you may be facing.

Affirmations for Anxious Attachment

Affirmations can be a valuable tool for individuals with anxious attachment tendencies to reduce anxiety, promote self-confidence, and foster healthier relationship patterns.

Here are some affirmations tailored specifically for anxious attachment:

- I am worthy of love and security in my relationships, just as I am.
- I trust that I can handle uncertainty and change in my relationships.
- I am not defined by my past experiences.
- I am capable of creating healthier attachments.
- I am deserving of love, respect, and kindness in all my relationships.
- I release the need for constant reassurance.
- I trust in the strength of my connections.
- I am secure in myself, and my worth is not dependent on external validation.
- I communicate my needs and boundaries clearly and assertively.
- I am resilient and can bounce back from my relationship challenges and grow stronger.
- I am learning to be patient and let love unfold naturally in my relationships.
- I release the fear of abandonment.
- I am open to receiving love and affection without reservation.

- I am working on creating loving and secure attachments with those I care about.
- I choose to focus on the present rather than worry about the future.
- I am becoming more secure in my attachments with each passing day.

To use these affirmations effectively to help you challenge those negative thoughts, consider the following tips:

1. Repeat these affirmations daily, to reinforce positive thought patterns. Be consistent.

2. Say them with genuine belief and conviction. Internalizing the affirmations is key to their effectiveness. Believe what you are saying.

3. Tailor these affirmations to your specific situation and feelings. Make them your own and personalize them to suit your needs.

4. Consider keeping a journal to track your progress and reflect on how these affirmations impact your thoughts and behaviors.

Remember that changing attachment patterns and reducing anxiety takes time and effort. Be patient with yourself and use these affirmations as part of a broader strategy for personal growth and developing healthier, more secure relationships.

Affirmations for Everyday

Affirmations for everyday life can help boost your self-confidence, maintain a positive mindset, and stay focused on your goals. Here are some great affirmations to incorporate into your daily routine:

- I am strong.
- I am worthy of love, success and happiness.
- I am in control of my thoughts and actions.
- I am capable of handling whatever comes my way today.
- I am grateful for the new day and the many opportunities it brings.
- I approach challenges with a positive and open mindset.
- I attract positive energy and people into my life.
- I am the architect of my own destiny.
- I release all negativity from yesterday and focus on the possibilities of today.
- I am at peace with my past, present, and future.
- I am resilient and bounce back from any setbacks with grace and determination.
- I am surrounded by love and support from friends and family.

- I prioritize self-care and take time for my well-being each day.
- I am a magnet for success and it flows effortlessly into my life.
- I am open to new opportunities and embrace change with enthusiasm.
- I am grateful for the abundance that life offers me.

Affirmations are more likely to help you change your negative thought patterns when spoken aloud, and are most effective in the morning or before bedtime. Write them down in a journal or on sticky notes, and choose a select few to use as a screensaver or background on your phone or computer. The key to the effectiveness of affirmations is consistency and a genuine belief in the positive statements. Affirmations can help improve your mindset and outlook on life.

Affirmations for Couples

In a relationship where one partner has an anxious attachment style, using affirmations can be a supportive and constructive way to foster security, trust, and understanding between both partners. These affirmations can be said by both individuals to help create a more secure and loving bond:

1. For the partner with anxious attachment:

- I trust in my partner's love and commitment to our relationship.
- I am secure in our love, even when my anxieties arise.
- I am capable of self-soothing and managing my anxiety.
- I am deserving of love and can accept it without fear.
- I communicate my needs and feelings openly and honestly.
- I am working on healing and creating a secure attachment.

2. For the partner providing support:

- I am patient and understanding of my partner's attachment style.
- I am committed to helping my partner feel secure in our relationship.
- I provide a safe and loving space for my partner to express their emotions.
- I respect my partner's boundaries and needs.
- I communicate my love and affection consistently.
- I support my partner's journey toward greater emotional security.

3. Joint affirmations to say together:

- Our love is strong and we work together to overcome challenges.

- We communicate openly and lovingly, focusing on building trust everyday.
- We both deserve a loving and secure relationship.
- We are committed to understanding each other's needs and feelings.
- Our love grows stronger as we support each other's growth.

When using these affirmations, it's important for both partners to genuinely believe in and practice them. Repeating them regularly can help reinforce positive behaviors and attitudes in the relationship. Couples may find it beneficial to seek the guidance of a therapist or counselor who specializes in attachment issues to work through any challenges and promote a more secure and loving bond.

Visualization for Anxious Attachment

Another aspect of affirmation is visualization. Visualization is a mental technique that involves creating vivid mental images or scenarios to help individuals achieve their specific goals, reduce stress, improve performance, and manage their emotional states.

For those with anxious attachment, it can be a powerful tool as it taps into the mind's ability to influence emotions and behaviors through the power of imagination.

Here's how visualization can be effective in addressing the challenges of anxious attachment:

Emotional Regulation

Anxious attachment is characterized by intense emotional reactions. Practicing visualization can help regulate these emotions by imagining scenarios where you feel loved, secure, and confident. By repeatedly visualizing these positive experiences, you can retrain your emotional responses in times of anxiety.

Behavioral Changes

Anxious attachment can often lead to behaviors that push others away, like clinginess or constant reassurance-seeking. Visualization can be used to create mental images of healthier behaviors and interactions in relationships by mentally rehearsing these behaviors and building confidence by adopting them in real-life situations.

Self-Esteem and Self-Worth

Low self-esteem and a sense of unworthiness are common when you have an anxious attachment style. Visualization can help you visualize yourself as deserving of love and affection, which can boost self-esteem and self-worth over time.

Creating a Secure Internal Attachment Figure

Visualization can help you create a secure internal attachment figure or safe place within your mind. This can serve as a source of comfort and support during times of anxiety or distress and will, ultimately, reduce your need for external validation.

Reducing Anxiety and Stress
Visualization has the ability to induce relaxation and reduce anxiety by imagining calming and peaceful scenarios. By practicing visualization regularly, you can develop a greater sense of calm and resilience, making it easier to manage your anxious attachment-related anxiety.

Visualization can be a helpful tool, but it is important to note that it is not a standalone solution, and is best used in conjunction with other therapeutic approaches like cognitive behavioral therapy, guided meditation, and affirmations.

Visualization and Affirmations: A Combination Tool

Visualization and affirmations can be used together as an even more powerful tool to manage your anxious attachment. Combining these techniques can help you address your attachment-related issues more comprehensively and effectively than they would be on their own.

Here's how they can work together:

Visualization

This involves creating vivid mental images or scenarios. To combat your anxious attachment and manage your attachment-related anxieties, you can visualize scenarios that promote secure attachment.

These include:

- Visualizing yourself in a relationship where you feel secure, loved, and valid.
- Imagining yourself reacting calmly and confidently in situations that typically trigger attachment anxiety.
- Creating mental images of positive interactions with others, where you are comfortable and at ease.

Affirmations

Combined with visualization, affirmations can enhance the effectiveness of the practice.

Here are a few affirmations that can complement visualization and help you manage your anxious attachment more effectively:

- I am worthy of love and security in my relationship

- I trust myself and my ability to navigate relationships with confidence
- I am capable of developing healthy and secure attachments
- I release my fear of abandonment and embrace a sense of self-assurance

Now that we have identified how each of these tools differs, and looked at what they entail, let's now look at how you can incorporate the techniques together.

Putting Visualizations and Affirmations into Practice

Step 1: Set the Intention

Start by setting a clear intention for your visualization and affirmation practice. What specific aspect of your anxious attachment are you working on? Are you looking to increase your sense of security, reduce anxiety, or improve your self-esteem in your relationships? Knowing your goal is half the battle, so identify it from the get-go.

Clearly state your intention. A good example of this is:
- "I want to improve my self-esteem and boost my confidence in my relationship"
- "I want to feel more secure in my relationship"

Step 2: Visualization

Close your eyes and start your visualization exercise. Remember to choose a quiet, comfortable spot where you won't be disturbed. Imagine the scenarios and situations that reflect your desired attachment style and the emotions you are trying to cultivate. While visualizing, immerse yourself in the sensory details and emotions associated with the scenarios.

If you are visualizing to improve your sense of security, visualize a time in your relationship when you felt secure. This could be you reflecting on a past date or event where your triggers and anxiety were completely at bay.

Step 3: Affirmations

Once you have visualized your ideal scenario of what you want to achieve, transition into your affirmations. Repeat affirmations that align with your goals. You can use those from the list above, or come up with your own that suit your goals more. Say them out loud and try to connect with the positive emotions and beliefs that these affirmations represent.

Here are a few affirmations that could be helpful:

- "I feel secure in my relationship"
- I am loved
- My partner will not simply abandon me

Step 4: Repeat Regularly

Consistency is key when trying to manage or overcome your anxious attachment. Practice this winning combination of visualization and affirmations regularly - ideally on a daily basis. The more you do it, the more they can help you rewire those negative thought patterns and beliefs about attachment and move on to forming secure attachments.

Step 5: Monitor Your Progress

The final step in this technique is to keep track of your progress over time. Notice any changes in your thoughts, feelings, and behaviors, and adjust your affirmations and visualizations as needed to address specific challenges or areas of improvement. Combining visualization and affirmations can be a valuable self-help tool for managing anxious attachment.

Keeping a journal or logging your progress will help you keep track of whether or not visualization is working for you.

There is power in visualizing and speaking out loud what you want to achieve as you try to manage and modify your thinking, emotions, and behaviors. And while it may seem silly to sit and say seemingly random sentences out loud, there is value in doing so. Ever heard the saying, "Don't knock it until you've tried it?" Well, this is the time to put aside any feelings of silliness and try a technique that is known to work.

Harmonious Healing: Affirmations and Visualizations in Practice

If you need a little more convincing that affirmations and visualization can, indeed, help you manage your attachment-related anxiety and help you change those negative thought patterns into positive ones, then this next case study is just for you as we take you through the real-life journey of one of the world's most influential women - Oprah Winfrey.

Oprah has never been one to shy away from talking about her past, and often shares her life story to encourage others to persevere and take control of their lives and trauma and turn it into something positive.

Having faced many personal challenges throughout her life, including childhood trauma, abuse, and self-worth and self-esteem issues, Ms. Winfrey used the power of affirmations and visualization to overcome her tumultuous past and move toward healing.

Here's how she did it.

Early Trauma

Oprah's extremely challenging childhood included poverty, abuse, and instability. From racial and gender discrimination to becoming pregnant at only fourteen as a result of sexual assault, Oprah went through horrors some of us can only imagine.

It was soon after this that she began using affirmations to cope with her circumstances. She would often repeat positive statements to herself, such as "I am special" and "I am going to prove them wrong."

Visualization

Oprah regularly practiced visualization techniques where she would imagine herself as a successful and empowered woman, hosting her own television program and using her platform to make a positive impact on the world. This, in turn, helped her overcome those feelings of unworthiness and that she was unloved. Visualization helped her stay focused on her goals.

Consistency

Oprah was consistent in her use of affirmations and visualization, using them as tools for self-motivation and empowerment that led to personal growth and emotional resilience throughout her adolescence and into her adult life.

The Results

In Oprah's case, the results of visualization and affirmations speak for themselves. Her dedication to affirmations and visualization played a significant role in her personal development and success. And despite her challenging upbringing, and the effects of this, she went on to achieve remarkable accomplishments with the Oprah Winfrey Show, Harpo Productions, and her philanthropic initiatives that include her school for girls in South Africa.

Oprah's story demonstrates how the consistent use of affirmations and visualization can help individuals overcome their personal hardships, build self-confidence, and achieve remarkable success. Her example also underscores the importance of resilience and self-belief in the face of adversity.

While it would be unfair to say that Oprah has an anxious attachment style, as we are not professionals or therapists that can diagnose this attachment style, we can guess that the many things she went through, including the neglect she faced as a child, may have given rise to feelings of fear of abandonment, insecurity, and the possibility of reacting irrationally to certain situations.

But, as her inspirational story shows, it is possible to overcome your anxious attachment and go on to lead a full and happy life that consists of secure attachments and fulfilling relationships.

Chapter Eight: Guided Meditation: The Path to Transforming Your Anxious Attachment

ଓଳ

Guided meditation forms a significant part of the transformation process, and is a powerful technique that has the ability to heal the deep emotional wounds that come with anxious attachment. It offers a structured, guided journey within your own mind, providing a sanctuary where you can confront and reframe those negative thought patterns.

Research into guided meditation has shown that it can positively affect the brain's structure and function, often increasing the volume of gray matter in those regions associated with self-awareness and emotional regulation.

Thanks to technology and the creation of guided meditation mobile applications, you can explore the world of guided meditation just about anywhere - at home, on your daily commute, or anywhere you have a few minutes alone. Headspace, Eckhart Tolle, and The Mindfulness Movement are the top three YouTube channels that you can use for your guided meditation session. Alternatively, you can download the

Headspace app on your Android or iPhone device from the app store.

Meditation Oasis is another resource that provides guided meditation and podcasts on the subject.

Here's what guided meditation can do for you and your anxious attachment:

1. Teaches you self-compassion
It's no secret that individuals with anxious attachment are their own worst enemies, often criticizing every aspect of their emotions and thoughts. Guided meditation can teach you to be gentle and compassionate towards yourself, fostering that all-important self-worth and acceptance. There is power in consistently hearing affirming and loving words during meditation, and is when you begin to internalize these messages and truly believe them.

2. Challenging those negative thought patterns
One of the biggest challenges that you may face as a result of your anxious attachment is the onslaught of negative thought patterns that seemingly take over from time to time. During guided meditation, you'll be encouraged to identify and challenge these negative thought patterns while gently

redirecting their focus. You can, and will, break free from this anxious thinking with the help of guided meditation.

3. Building resilience

Emotional resilience is often the key to overcoming your anxious attachment, and meditations encourage this by helping you become more attuned to your emotions and to process your feelings without becoming overwhelmed. This emotional resilience allows for healthier reactions and behaviors in your relationships with your partner, friends, and family.

4. Mindful relationship building

Anxious attachment sufferers can learn to develop a mindful approach to relationships through guided meditation as they become aware of their needs and boundaries and how to communicate these more effectively. Making choices that align with your well-being might not be easy, but it can be learned with guided meditation.

A Few Notes about Guided Meditation

Before we jump into our "how-to" section on guided meditation, it is necessary to first note a few things about what to expect and how to implement it into your healing journey.

- Guided meditations can form a healthy part of your routine. We encourage you to try it as often as possible and see what a difference it can make
- Start with short sessions and extend them when you become more comfortable
- Find a quiet, comfortable space away from any distractions
- Use headphones to help you focus and minimize distractions
- Be fully present in your guided meditation session

Guided meditation can be a powerful tool when used correctly, and can help you rewrite the script of anxious attachment that aids in building the secure, loving relationship that you deserve.

Guided Meditation - How to Do It

Here's how you can do guided meditation in the comfort of your own home to help you change your negative thought patterns and overcome your anxious attachment:

Before you start, find a quiet and comfortable space where you won't be disturbed or distracted. Sit on a chair or on the floor with your back straight and your hands resting gently in your lap. Close your eyes and take a few deep breaths to center yourself before you follow these steps:

Step 1: Set your intention

Start by setting a clear intention for your meditation. Visualize what it is you are hoping to gain from your guided meditation, whether it be the feeling of a secure attachment or just generally improved mental well-being.

Step 2: Do a body scan

Take a minute to "scan" your body for any tension or discomfort. Start with your head, taking note of any niggles or pain, and move down your body to your toes. If there is in fact tension, imagine it melting away with every exhale. Many people tend to hold their stress in their jaw and shoulders, so spend extra time on these areas.

Step 3: Ground yourself

Grounding yourself is vitally important in any guided meditation session, and can be done by imagining that roots are extending from the soles of your feet and going deep into the earth. These roots anchor you firmly in the ground and give you stability and connection to the present.

Step 4: Breathing

Shift your focus to your breathing as you notice the natural rhythm of every breath you take. This can be an excellent point of focus as you take cognizance of every breath entering and leaving your body. Should your mind start to wander, gently bring it back to focus on your breathing.

Step 5: Acknowledging your anxious attachment
Now is the time to bring your awareness to those negative thought patterns that dictate your attachment style. Allow yourself to acknowledge these thoughts. Fear of abandonment, self-doubt, and insecurity are all common thoughts that you may have, so recognize them without judgment.

Step 6: Self-compassion
With your eyes still closed, imagine a warm, loving light surrounding your entire body. This light represents the compassion and self-love that you deserve. Let it envelop you, leaving you with a feeling of acceptance and worthiness. Repeat the following affirmations while doing so: "I am worthy of love." "I am worthy of security." "I am not my anxious attachment."

Step 7: Reframe your negative thoughts
Imagine each negative thought as a leaf floating down a stream. Watch them float away and let go of these negative thoughts and beliefs as you do so. Replace the negative with positive thoughts, again repeating your affirmations.

Step 8: Embrace security

Visualize yourself in a loving and secure relationship, imagining the feelings of safety, trust, and contentment that come with it. Imagine yourself confidently expressing your needs and boundaries while feeling accepted and loved by your partner.

Step 9: Gratitude
Take a second to express gratitude for the sense of security and self-worth that your meditation session has brought, and feel the joy that this gratitude has brought.

Step 10: Closing the meditation
Once again, focus on your breathing. Take a few deep breaths and bring your attention to your physical surroundings. This last step is an important one, so take as much time as you need before you gently open your eyes and bring your guided meditation session to a close.

Remember, healing and growth take time, so be patient and kind to yourself as you focus on your very important journey to overcoming your anxious attachment.

CBT and Guided Meditation: A Winning Solution

Cognitive behavioral therapy offers a powerful framework for overcoming your anxious attachment and can help you recognize the negative thought patterns and behaviors that do more harm to your relationships. Consistency is key, so keep writing in your journal, identify any common triggers and behaviors, and work on each as they happen rather than ignoring them and ultimately being faced with a bigger problem.

Guided meditation, too, has the power to help you change your behavior for good, instilling in you a positive mindset that can help you conquer the challenges of anxious attachment and change your negative thought patterns and behaviors for good.

You have the power and the ability to change your thinking and overcome your anxious attachment. And cognitive behavior therapy is the toolkit that can help you do so.

Conclusion

As we reach the final chapter of this journey through the many challenges and intricacies of anxious attachment, we want to congratulate you on making it through to the end. Whether you are someone with anxious attachment, or are a partner, friend or family member trying to understand and support your loved one with empathy and care, your commitment to learning and growing is commendable.

The road we have traveled together has been filled with insights, emotions, and challenges - and let's not forget the valuable tips that we have shared. We've explored the inner workings of anxious attachment, delving deep into the origins of these negative thought patterns and the way they shape our relationships.

But, as we now conclude our journey, we want to offer you a message of hope. Living with anxious attachment can be incredibly challenging, with the constant oscillation between the need for closeness and the fear of rejection, it's enough to make you feel like you are on an emotional rollercoaster. And while your partner, friends and family might have been confused and perplexed by your actions and emotions, you can take comfort in knowing that you are not alone in your struggles.

It is vitally important to remember that anxious attachment is not a life sentence. It is not what defines you. It is simply a pattern of behavior that is rooted in past experiences and learned coping mechanisms. With the right tools, many of which we have shared throughout the chapters of this book, a bit of extra support and determination, you can rewrite your attachment narrative and move towards forming secure attachments.

To recap just a fraction of what we have learned, here is what we have covered:

1. The importance of self-awareness

The very first step towards change is self-awareness. Recognizing that you have an anxious attachment and understanding its origins, you have taken a significant and celebration-worthy stride. Continue to explore these emotions, your triggers, and negative thought patterns in a non-judgmental way.

2. Communication

Open and honest communication is truly the cornerstone of any healthy relationship, and is possibly the only way to learn to express your needs, fears, and desires to those in your life.

Encourage this same communication from your loved ones as you move towards building a more secure attachment.

3. Mindfulness and self-care

Work towards developing a mindfulness practice to help you stay grounded in the present moment. Whether it's through cognitive behavioral therapy or another approach that we have explored, self-care and practicing mindfulness are not selfish, and form the necessary foundations for building secure attachments. Prioritize your emotional and physical well-being first, and the rest will come together.

4. Challenge your negative beliefs

Challenging negative beliefs requires consistency. Rather than focusing on these negative thought patterns and beliefs, replace them with self-compassion and positive affirmations. You are worthy of love. You are worthy of compassion and understanding. You are not your anxious attachment, and you can learn how to form secure attachments.

5. Seek professional help

There may come a time when dealing with your anxious attachment requires the guidance of a professional. Take comfort in knowing that this is not a bad thing, and that there is no shame in admitting that you need a bit of help. Therapists, counselors, and support groups are all invaluable sources of assistance that can help you on your journey toward security.

6. The Value of Self-Help Therapies and Techniques

Self-help therapies and techniques can be immensely valuable for someone with an anxious attachment style. While therapy with a trained professional is often recommended for addressing the deep-rooted issues associated with attachment issues, self-help strategies can complement and enhance the therapeutic process, even replacing it in some cases. Self-help therapies can help you:

- Increase your self-awareness
- Empower you to take an active role in your personal growth and healing
- Give you a sense of control over your attachment-related challenges
- Teach you practical tools for managing anxiety and strong emotions independently
- Build your self-esteem
- Help you set and maintain healthy boundaries
- Assist you in developing coping strategies
- Encourage personal growth and development as you explore your interests, hobbies, and goals outside of your relationship

It is important to note that self-help resources are highly beneficial, but may not be a suitable replacement for those with severe attachment issues. If you feel that you need extra help, consult a healthcare professional who is trained to deal with attachment-related issues and who will help you discover the origins of your attachment and how to overcome the challenges of it.

7. Give it time

Change takes time. And you should not expect your anxious attachment to simply disappear overnight. Be patient with yourself and your progress, no matter how slow it may seem. Celebrate even the smallest victories, and don't be discouraged by any setbacks that are sure to crop up when you least expect them. This is truly a journey, so embrace it and keep at it even when you feel like giving up.

Anxious attachment may seem like it has a hold on your life and your relationships. But, it doesn't need to be this way. As the pages of this book have taught you, you are not your anxious attachment - it is merely a response to how your emotional needs were met, or unmet, in those early days when you were learning whom you could rely on for emotional comfort and who was not there for you.

To fully understand anxious attachment, we must first grasp its roots. Originating in early childhood, anxious attachment usually stems from not having your emotional needs met. This experience in turn shapes the core beliefs that you have about yourself and others, leading to an intense fear of abandonment, a constant need for reassurance, and an over-reliance on external validation.

The journey to resolving anxious attachment, as we have come to learn through the pages of this book, begins with self-awareness and the importance of recognizing and understanding your attachment style and how it manifests itself in your relationships.

Resolving your anxious attachment is not about erasing your attachment style, but rather transforming it into a more secure one. This is only possible if you are willing to put in the hard work and dedication that it takes to cultivate a sense of security within yourself as you learn to develop secure attachments with others.

For the partners, friends, and family members of those with anxious attachment, your presence and understanding are invaluable. Your willingness to learn and empathize while supporting your loved one through the challenges of their anxious attachment can make a world of difference. Remember, too, that no matter how hard you try, you cannot fix someone's attachment style, but you can help them along the way by providing a safe and supportive environment in which they can take comfort and heal.

As we now reach the end of our journey together, we want to once again emphasize that anxious attachment does not define you, nor does it dictate your future. With dedication and putting into practice the tips and strategies outlined in this book, you can break free from the shackles of insecurity and fear and learn to form secure attachments. The path ahead may be scary and challenging, but is it so undeniably worth it.

And as you apply these tips and techniques, you might just find that your relationships undergo a profound transformation. The cycle of anxious attachment can be broken, and this will lead to more secure, and fulfilling connections becoming the norm.

An insecure or anxious attachment pattern often leads to a dance of push-pull dynamics, with anxious attachers seeking closeness and avoidant attachers pulling away. Resolving, or rather challenging, your anxious attachment will help you be better equipped to create partnerships based on mutual trust, emotional intimacy, and interdependence.

Embrace the journey, one step at a time, and remember that you are deserving of love, stability, and happiness. Your future is bright, filled with the potential for secure, loving, and fulfilling relationships. Trust in your ability to change and grow, and may your heart find the security it so deeply craves.

We want to finish this book off with a powerful quote: *"Yes, love yourself. But also analyze and be critical of how you think, act and behave. Self-love without self-awareness is useless. Be accountable."* - Unknown

Author's Note

Dear Reader,

I want to express my sincere gratitude for choosing to read my book. I hope the knowledge and insights you've gained have been valuable and enriching.

If you found this book informative, or if it has helped you in any way, I kindly request that you take a moment to share your thoughts through a review (QR codes on the following page).

Your reviews not only provide essential feedback for me, but also assist future readers in making an informed decision. Whether you have a few sentences or a more detailed review to share, please consider letting others know about your experience with this book.

The motivation for writing this book was entirely personal. I have had my eyes opened to what anxious attachment is all about. I have nothing but empathy for those whose relationships are impacted by anxious attachment, but I also have nothing but confidence that those who are determined enough to make small, consistent improvements, will eventually find themselves considerably more secure.

Once again, thank you for being a part of this journey. I hope that you gained some value from it and I look forward to creating more quality content in the future.

Amazon.com	Amazon.co.uk
Amazon.ca	Amazon.com.au

References

A brief overview of adult attachment Theory and research | R. Chris Fraley. (n.d.).
http://labs.psychology.illinois.edu/~rcfraley/attachment.htm

Ackerman, C. E., MA. (2023, April 19). *What is Attachment Theory? Bowlby's 4 Stages Explained.* PositivePsychology.com. https://positivepsychology.com/attachment-theory/

Attachment styles. (n.d.). Attachment Styles.
https://scholar.harvard.edu/sociology1152/attachment-styles-0

Benoit, D. (2004). Infant-parent attachment: Definition, types, antecedents, measurement and outcome. *Paediatrics and Child Health, 9*(8), 541–545. https://doi.org/10.1093/pch/9.8.541

BetterHelp Editorial Team. (2023, October 20). *How To Manage An Anxious Attachment Style.*
https://www.betterhelp.com/advice/anxiety/ridding-yourself-of-attachment-anxiety/

Effa, C. (2023, September 26). *How can you fix an anxious attachment style?*

https://www.medicalnewstoday.com/articles/how-to-fix-anxious-attachment-style

Hakhmigari, M. K., Peled, Y., Krissi, H., Levy, S., Molmen-Lichter, M., & Handelzalts, J. E. (2021). Anxious attachment mediates the associations between early recollections of mother's own parental bonding and Mother–Infant bonding: a 2-Month Path Analysis model. *Frontiers in Psychiatry, 12.* https://doi.org/10.3389/fpsyt.2021.682161

How to Stop Attachment Insecurity from Ruining Your Love Life. (n.d.). Greater Good. https://greatergood.berkeley.edu/article/item/how_to_stop_attachment_insecurity_from_ruining_your_love_life

Lebow, H. I. (2022, June 22). *Anxious attachment style: Signs, causes, and how to change.* Psych Central. https://psychcentral.com/health/anxious-attachment-style-signs

Manson, M. (2023, March 15). Attachment styles and how they affect your relationships. *Mark Manson.* https://markmanson.net/attachment-styles

Mcleod, S., PhD. (2023). Attachment Theory In Psychology. *Simply Psychology.* https://www.simplypsychology.org/attachment.html

mindbodygreen. (2023, June 20). *Tend To Feel Insecure In Relationships? This Is Your Attachment Style.* Mindbodygreen. https://www.mindbodygreen.com/articles/anxious-attachment-style

MSc, O. G. (2023, October 30). *Anxious attachment style: What it looks like in adult relationships.* Simply Psychology. https://www.simplypsychology.org/anxious-attachment-style.html

MSEd, K. C. (2023, February 22). *What is attachment theory?* Verywell Mind. https://www.verywellmind.com/what-is-attachment-theory-2795337

Persensky, M. (2023, September 18). The 4 attachment styles and how they impact you. *Cleveland Clinic.* https://health.clevelandclinic.org/attachment-theory-and-attachment-styles/

PsyD, C. R. (2023, November 2). *Anxious attachment: How does it affect relationships?* Anxiety Disorders and Universal

Health Care. https://www.anxiety.org/anxious-attachment-how-parental-behavior-affects-adult-intimate-relationships

Read, D. L., Clark, G. I., Rock, A. J., & Coventry, W. L. (2018). Adult attachment and social anxiety: The mediating role of emotion regulation strategies. *PLOS ONE, 13*(12), e0207514. https://doi.org/10.1371/journal.pone.0207514

Sagone, E., Commodari, E., Indiana, M. L., & La Rosa, V. L. (2023). Exploring the Association between Attachment Style, Psychological Well-Being, and Relationship Status in Young Adults and Adults—A Cross-Sectional Study. *European Journal of Investigation in Health, Psychology and Education, 13*(3), 525–539. https://doi.org/10.3390/ejihpe13030040

Sheinbaum, T., Kwapil, T. R., Ballespí, S., Mitjavila, M., Chun, C. A., Silvia, P. J., & Barrantes-Vidal, N. (2015). Attachment style predicts affect, cognitive appraisals, and social functioning in daily life. *Frontiers in Psychology, 6*. https://doi.org/10.3389/fpsyg.2015.00296

Simpson, J. A., & Rholes, W. S. (2017). Adult attachment, stress, and romantic relationships. *Current Opinion in Psychology, 13*, 19–24. https://doi.org/10.1016/j.copsyc.2016.04.006

Team. (2023, June 5). *Anxious Attachment Style Guide: Causes & symptoms*. Attachment Project. https://www.attachmentproject.com/blog/anxious-attachment/

Vowels, L. M., Carnelley, K. B., & Stanton, S. C. E. (2022). Attachment anxiety predicts worse mental health outcomes during COVID-19: Evidence from two studies. *Personality and Individual Differences, 185*, 111256. https://doi.org/10.1016/j.paid.2021.111256

WebMD Editorial Contributors. (2011, April 9). *What is anxious attachment?* WebMD. https://www.webmd.com/mental-health/what-is-anxious-attachment

Printed in Great Britain
by Amazon